meaw

Jack

Ivy

Scrapbooking Your Pets

Scrapbooking Your Pets

200 Page Designs

Stacey Panassidi

Sterling Publishing Co., Inc. New York

A Sterling/Chapelle Book

Chapelle, Ltd., Inc., P.O. Box 9252, Ogden, UT 84409
(801) 621-2777 • (801) 621-2788 Fax
e-mail: chapelle@chapelleltd.com
Web site: www.chapelleltd.com

Library of Congress Cataloging-in-Publication Data available:

Panassidi, Stacey.
  Scrapbooking your pets : 200 page designs / Stacey Panassidi.
    p. cm.
  "A Sterling/Chapelle Book."
  Includes index.
  ISBN 1-4027-1657-5
1. Photographs--Conservation and restoration. 2. Photograph
albums. 3. Scrapbooks. 4. Pets. I. Title.
  TR465.P36 2005
  745.593--dc22

                                               2005008744

10 9 8 7 6 5 4 3 2 1
Published by Sterling Publishing Co., Inc.
387 Park Avenue South, New York, NY 10016
©2005 by Stacey Panassidi
Distributed in Canada by Sterling Publishing
c/o Canadian Manda Group, 165 Dufferin Street
Toronto, Ontario, Canada M6K 3H6
Distributed in Great Britain by Chrysalis Books Group PLC,
The Chrysalis Building, Bramley Road, London W10 6SP, England
Distributed in Australia by Capricorn Link (Australia) Pty. Ltd.
P. O. Box 704, Windsor, NSW 2756, Australia
Printed and Bound in China
All Rights Reserved

Sterling ISBN 1-4027-1657-5

Table of Contents

Savannah and Trevor enjoying a typical summer's day

SAMPLE

INSPECT

DIG IN

Dig In

Man's Best Friend

If you have a dog, you know that they are fabulous pets. They become an integral part of your family. So why not include these beloved animals in your scrapbook? You can capture your pet in relaxed moments, typical settings, or with friends or family members. Create layouts that make you laugh. Haven't we all dressed up our dogs at some point? These beautiful animals enrich our lives. Tell the story of how your paths crossed—did you adopt your dog or did one of your neighbors give you a puppy? In the following pages, you will be inspired by the ways the designers have included these beloved pets into their layouts.

No matter how little money and how few possessions you own, having a dog makes you rich.

Louie & Mickie

secrets

Man's Best Friend

Louie ♥ Mickie

L O U I S ♥ M I C K I E

Louis and Mickie understood each other. It was a relationship filled with mutual respect and
admiration. There was often a 'knowing' look that past between the two of them of a secret
shared at the garage which no one else was privy to. Both Mickie and Louis have left us for
places that we cannot yet travel to. I wonder, even now, if they are together, sharing secrets
But I know for certain that, we are the better, because both of them were in our lives.

Remember

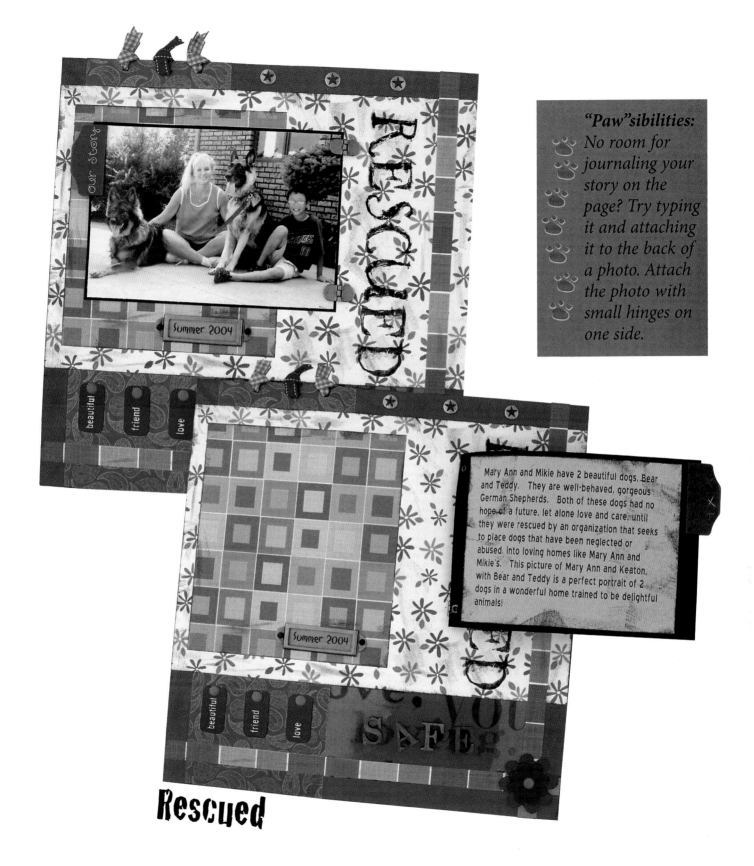

RESCUED

Our story

Summer 2004

beautiful friend love

"Paw"sibilities: *No room for journaling your story on the page? Try typing it and attaching it to the back of a photo. Attach the photo with small hinges on one side.*

Summer 2004

beautiful friend love

Mary Ann and Mikie have 2 beautiful dogs, Bear and Teddy. They are well-behaved, gorgeous German Shepherds. Both of these dogs had no hope of a future, let alone love and care, until they were rescued by an organization that seeks to place dogs that have been neglected or abused, into loving homes like Mary Ann and Mikie's. This picture of Mary Ann and Keaton, with Bear and Teddy is a perfect portrait of 2 dogs in a wonderful home trained to be delightful animals!

Rescued

Blue-eyed Relay

Cherish

Play Time

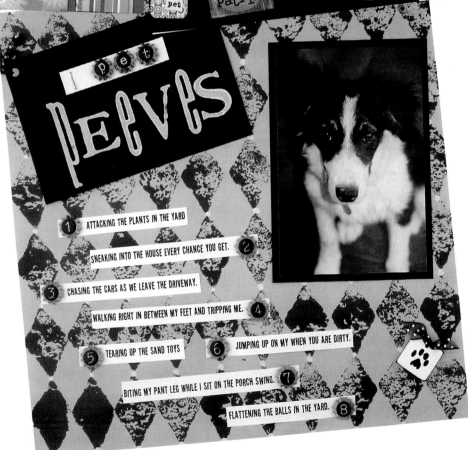

Pet Peeves

1. ATTACKING THE PLANTS IN THE YARD
2. SNEAKING INTO THE HOUSE EVERY CHANCE YOU GET.
3. CHASING THE CARS AS WE LEAVE THE DRIVEWAY.
4. WALKING RIGHT IN BETWEEN MY FEET AND TRIPPING ME.
5. TEARING UP THE SAND TOYS
6. JUMPING UP ON MY WHEN YOU ARE DIRTY.
7. BITING MY PANT LEG WHILE I SIT ON THE PORCH SWING.
8. FLATTENING THE BALLS IN THE YARD.

Pet Tails:
Dogs are pack animals by nature. They need closeness, touching, and petting to be content and happy.

Pet Peeves

Backyard Adventure

A BOY & HIS DOG

BACKYARD ADVENTURE

Always Together

TOGETHER

Puppy Promenade

M. LAND

It was such a fun summer day when I took Blitz over to my niece's house for the first time to play! There were tons of kids to run around with and a few other dogs too! I snapped this adorable picture when my niece Emma decided she wanted to dance with Blitz. At close to six months old, he is the perfect size for her right now. I am not sure how Blitz felt about dancing, but Emma had a blast! I do know that when Blitz came home that afternoon he needed a LONG nap!

Puppy Promenade

"Paw"sibilities: Have your sewing scrap basket on hand when you are scrapbooking. Buttons and trims are fun additions to your pages.

Dad's Li'l Buddy

FRIEND

['frend] **Ff**

synonyms: buddy, partner, intimate, confidant, familiar, acquaintance, mate, cater-cousin, side kick

see: amigo, best friend, alter-ego, ally, colleague

LOVE

Dad's Lil Buddy

Pet Tails: A one-year-old dog is physically as mature as a 15-year-old human.

Dad and I have always had a very special relationship as father and daughter. We're two peas in a pod in so many ways. He brings me a lot of joy. One of the things I've tremendously enjoyed is watching him interact with my dog, Malachi.

Now, these two do not act like "man" and "dog", rather, they act like two little boys. One moment they may be wrestling and teasing each other and the next moment, they will be cuddling. I happened to catch them when they were cuddling and was able to take these photos.

Dad loves this little dog; this little dog loves Dad! When Malachi hears my Dad outside, his ears perk up and he waits at the door until my Dad comes in. Once Dad is in the house, Malachi is there begging for a tousle or a hug, whichever comes first.

Best of Buddies

Bailey & Jim

believe · strength · believe · integrity · believ

FureY ReUnioN '04

The Best of BUDDIEs

The best of friends

bailey and jim

Pet Tails:
If someone in the house is allergic to dogs, bathe your pet once a week. They will slough off less dead skin. It also helps to add a teaspoon of cooking oil to their dog food.

doG dIctIonaRy

TANNER TANNER TANNER TANNER TANNER

bath A PROCESS BY WHICH HUMANS DRENCH THE FLOOR, WALLS AND THEMSELVES. YOU CAN HELP BY SHAKING VIGOROUSLY

T

Dog Dictionary

a **dog** has a to bestow his **heart**

John • Dad • maLAChi

SUMMER 04

to bestow his **heart**

Faithful Friendship

"Paw"sibilities:
Sometimes one special photo is all you need on a page. Make certain it is a good quality photo and enlarge it as much as you can.

Taylor received Daisy on his 4th Birthday and they have been inseparable ever since. They play together, watch TV and have hours of fun chasing each other around the yard. Everyone told us every little boy should have a dog to call his own, but they didn't warn us that they would see the bond between Taylor and Daisy.

Calli

Best Friend

COMPANION SWEET FRIENDLY LOVING

Man's Best Friend

I am not sure that my husband would describe our dog as his best friend at this point in time. We have never had a larger breed dog before so this is a new experience for all of us. My husband Igel is very frustrated with Blitz because he is so hyperactive and does not listen well. I think it is hard for him to think of Blitz as a puppy still because he is larger than any full grown dog we have ever owned. He is only six months old and is all VERY full of energy! I think if we had a smaller breed six month old puppy my husband would be much more patient with it. I know once Blitz grows up and mellows out a little he and my husband will have a great relationship. My husband has always had a fondness for animals and I know Blitz will be no exception! I can already see in these pictures that this relationship is already starting to form.

woof

We Are Family

WE aRe FAMILY

TOGETHERNESS (to-geth'-ur-nes) 1. the spending of much time together, resulting in a more unified bond

Leah Noel
aka Leah Lou

Gives kisses
Jealous
Wants constant attention
Protector of the family
Would play ball ALL DAY!
Eats the wings off of Cicada bugs

Brandy Boo
aka The Gidge

Loves to eat
Her beak makes noises
Snores loudly
Likes to hang with the big dogs
Just wants to be loved!

Chewbacca Lestat
aka Chunk

Teddy Bear and Snuggle Bug
Thinks he is human
Loves to go for car rides
And have the wind in his face
Extremely possessive
Suffers from separation anxiety

Pet Tails:
The reason a dog has so many friends is that he wags his tail instead of his tongue.
—unknown

My Dog

Buddies

Our Sweet Girl

Calli's Album

12·15·01

C

puppy love

i love u

woof

LOVE

Calli

cool in the Pool

relax

cool in

p

You are also an excellent swimmer! You love to dive under the water to catch a ball or a ring! You are the best pool-toy!

"Paw"sibilities: Create fun tags to journal on, then tuck them behind the photos to create a little interaction on your page.

Pet Tails:
The dog was specially created for children. He is the god of frolic.
—Henry Ward Beecher

Man's Best Friend
Ethan & Bommer-Fall 2002

D Is for Dog

"Paw"sibilities: Zippers make great accents for your pages. Notice on the page at left how the unzipped portion reveals part of the title.

Summer Splash

Love You to Pieces

LOVE YOU TO PIECES

kiersten and g...

Hippie Chick

We realized that Sandy was in desperate need of a hair cut so I set up a grooming appointment for her. Her hair was so long and looked uncomfortable in the summer heat. Steve and the kids took her down and after a few hours picked up the new and improved Sandy. She looked so happy to be clean and trimmed. We let her stay in our house for a couple hours that evening and she acted like inside was where she belonged... part of our family... in our home... just like one of us.

before

after SaNdy wAs oNe HIPPIE CHICK

Aug 14th

Newborn LOVE

As my brother welcomed home his new baby, so did their dog. They worried that the dog would be jealous. They had nothing to worry about. Their dog fell in love with baby immediately, and even went over to give the baby a welcoming kiss hello!

may 2004

Pet Tails:
In America, one family in three owns at least one dog.

Newborn Love

Hula Pup

Meet Pucci the amazing

Hula Pup

You're the life of the luau!

Savannah, Sheree, & Pucci 8-04

Canine Companion

Kyle & Nyah

canine companion

Fall 2002

puppy

friend

Kiera

KIERA

Pet Tails: *All dogs, from the German Shepherd to the tiny Poodle, are direct descendants of wolves. They can all breed together and produce fertile offspring. Technically, they are all the same species.*

Snow Day

"Paw"sibilities: Hand- or machine-stitch your photos onto the page. This is a great way to make a pocket for a pull-out tag.

Taylor and Daisy had such a blast playing in the snow! I had to make them come in after playing outside for hours. Daisy's whiskers were frozen solid from all the snow she was eating and Taylor's cheeks were as red as could be but it didn't seem to deter either of them from wanting to go right back out after they had warmed up a bit.

Little Miss Priss

little **Miss** Priss

NOT!

There you sit with your paws crossed, acting like the perfect little lady. Leah you know how to pose for the camera and put on quite the act. But those of us who know and love you are very well aware that that is exactly what it is — an ACT! The real Leah is 100%

tom boy!

Pet Tails: The average dog lives to be about 15 years old.

Tanner

T A N N E R

Dogs are **forever** in the moment. They are always a tidal wave of **feelings**, and every feeling is some variant of **love**.

Pals

Pet Tails:
A dog is the only thing on earth that loves you more than he loves himself.
—Josh Billings

A dog is the only thing on this earth that loves you more than he loves himself.
-Josh Billings

PALS

faithful

loyal

UNSELFISH

impawsible

BEST Friends

KING of the YaRD

my Shadow

DOGGY DAYS

the face I love

it's a dog's life

Perfect

man's Best Friend

M A X

Every Dog

EVERY DOG

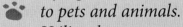
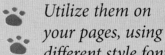

HAS ITS Day

"Paw"sibilities:
There are many sayings that relate to pets and animals. Utilize them on your pages, using different style fonts.

Pet Tails:
You think dogs will not be in heaven? I tell you they will be there long before any of us.
—Robert Louis Stevenson

Friend

Kooky

Savannah
AKA Piggy Princess

PLAY Ball

anner AND Susan

TANNER LOVES TO PLAY WITH TENNIS BALLS — I DON'T THINK HE WOULD EVER TIRE OF IT! HE GETS SO EXCITED AT THE IDEA OF GOING OUT TO PLAY EVEN IF...

Family

Play Ball

Pet Tails: *Don't attempt to teach your dog anything else until he can sit and stay on command for at least one minute.*

Mona Lisa

sleepy like this, he is deceptively innocent

Here Kitty Kitty

If you have a kitten, then you have many things to scrapbook. Kittens are the cutest creatures, and they are always in trouble. Never leave a shoelace unattended, or a thread hanging from a sleeve, because your kitten will surely be playing with it. Does your kitten have a favorite hiding spot, or do you have an entire litter of kitties? They grow so fast! Don't miss the milestones of your kitten's life; include them in your layouts as the designers did in the following chapter.

It is impossible to keep a straight face in the presence of one or more kittens.
—Cynthia E. Varnado

Kitty in a Box

Gray Kitty

Feline Friend

Keisha & Princess

Animals are such
agreeable friends-
they ask no questions,
they pass no
criticisms. G. Eliot

KEISHA AND PRINCESS

Ashlee & Amos

A
S
H
L
E
E
&
AMOS

A

FRIENDS

"Paw"sibilities:
Rubber Stamping, like the foam flower stamps used above, is a fun way to tie everything together once the page has been laid out.

Kisses

kisses from kitten

Nina's favorite things? Of course the first thing on the list is kisses from Jack! —2004

n & j

Pet Tails:
Kittens are born with their eyes closed. When they open, they will always be blue first. They change colors over a period of months to the final eye color.

Peek-a-Boo Kitties

peek a BOO KITTIES

may 04

On this day the kitties looked so sweet peeking their little heads out of the hole in the garage. Our kittens have always been a bit timid of us, so when we would try to get closer to them, they would back up into the garage. It has been so much fun to watch the personalities of our kittens develop and see their playfulness come out. I hope they become more comfortable with us and allow us get a little closer next time.

Newborn Kittens

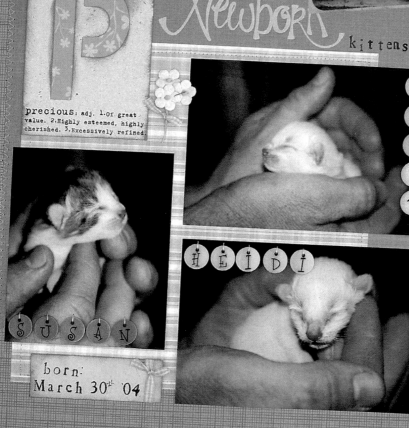

Newborn kittens

precious: adj. 1.Of great value. 2.Highly esteemed, highly cherished. 3.Excessively refined.

CINDY

HEIDI

SUSAN

born: March 30th '04

COUCH KITTY

WHAT IS big, FAT, yellow, AND LAZY AND USES THE COUCH
AS HIS OWN PERSONAL LOUNGING ... THOMAS! WHETHER
HE'S STRETCHED OUT SO THAT T...
DOWN OR HE'S USING THE BACK...
THE WINDOWSILL, THOMAS IS DEF...

Couch Kitty

Pet Tails: If you want the best seat in the house, remove the cat.

Three Little Kittens

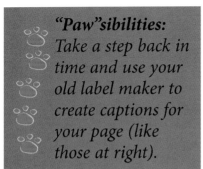

"Paw"sibilities: Take a step back in time and use your old label maker to create captions for your page (like those at right).

CAP'N

SPARROW

THE PIRATE CAT

DEVIOUS

SWASHBUCKLER

DARING

RAKISH

BRAVE

PLUNDERER

MUTINOUS

WILD

MISCHIEVOUS

DEVILISH

SWAGGERING

PILLAGER

CUNNING

THE PIRATES' LIFE FOR ME

YO HO

YO HO

Patience

It's an irony that does not esca...
girl who walks; she skips & danc...
sits; she pounces & wiggles. She ...
enough to watch a Sponge Bob ...
she's quiet. She isn't moving at all. She has
maintained this stillness over an hour.
Shhh! Ivy is napping.
She doesn't want to disturb her.

When Rose was tired, she read to her from a picture- and when the lunch- was opened, she fed her with a and an and some. And by and by the cars stopped, and Betty saw the SEASIDE, over the door of the station. "Oh, oh," she cried, "we are here!" And there was Aunt Alice on the platform, and Bert with his and oh, oh, there was cunning Carrie right behind them! Betty was so excited that she forgot everything. She tumbled off the car into Aunt Alice's. Ding, dong! went the , round went the , the train moved off slowly...

PATIENCE

Cat Eyes

Pet Tails: You can tell a cat's mood by looking into its eyes. A frightened or excited cat will have large, round pupils. An angry cat will have narrow pupils.

Kitty Fishing

Here Kitty

absolute craziness. that's what occurs when you combine my husband, some yarn and my cat. it's also commonly referred to as "kitty fishing." thomas hides — usually in a box — and casts his line of yarn and waits for thomas to react. soon, all that remains is a kitty wrapped in yarn like a package and a cackling with laughter husband. what crazy boys!

Pet Tails: Cats who are not around people the first three months of life, usually don't make good pets.

Kitty Gingivitis

4. We recommend at this time treating Thomas' gingivitis with a topical chlorhexidine gel. Please brush Thomas' teeth each day massaging the gel onto the teeth and gums continue this for 3-4 weeks.

351445 THOMAS
BAUER, MELANIE

Diagnosis :
Juvenile Kitty Gingivitis

Ivy & Blythe

Pet Tails:
Cats have five toes on their front paws and four toes on their back paws.

Christmas Cutie

MOBY CHRISTMAS CUTIE

THERE WAS SOMETHING FASCINATING ABOUT THE BAG OF XMAS LIGHTS

PRECIOUS

"Paw"sibilities:
Don't forget to include your pets in your holiday scrapbooking. Keep your camera on hand for those perfect photo opportunities.

christmas '03

thomas became a royal terror around christmas. the tree falls, ornaments go missing and twinkling lights are appetizers. thomas especially loves the christmas tree skirt that uncle chuck and aunt debbie gave us as a wedding gift. it's quilted and makes for a nice warm bed. this year he took his activities to a new extreme. we had just taken the tree down when thomas replaced the empty void in the skirt with himself. this went on for three days before we were finally able to put the tree skirt away for next year.

Kitty Christmas

One, Two Kitty

one, two

Kitty²

CATS CATS CATS CATS CATS CATS CATS CATS CATS

excited that his

Sable

Summer 2003

loved.

I Scrapped the Cat

SCRAPPED

the

MEOW

Boots

SEPT • 04

wonder

curiosity

explore

Puppy Love

They Call It Puppy Love

Having a puppy is like having a new baby. You must train them, stop them from biting, and teach them to sit and listen. You also have to love them unconditionally, because there will be moments when you will be pretty crazy! A puppy can destroy a house in a matter of moments, yet your home would feel empty without them. That puppy will grow into a beloved member of your family, so make sure to capture their cutest moments in your scrapbook!

Whoever said you can't buy happiness,
forgot about little puppies.

–Gene Hill

Full House

FULL HOUSE

How Much?

How much is that Puppy?

dog outfit $29.99

dog toys $9.99

stuffed dog $35.99

dog bed $14.99

Loving Your Puppy...

Priceless

"Paw"sibilities:
Use a small file folder to make a scrapbook of your pet. The staples, paper clips, and labels used in this layout carry out the "file folder" theme.

Sylvester

Every Dog Has Its Day

EVERY DOG

HAS IT'S Day

BABY BUCK

lift

OCCASION: Picking Out a New Puppy   NOTES: Birthday
DATE 4 days before Steves

Getting a new puppy was the only
thing Steve wanted...

...agreed to keep him for a few days
for the suprise! On Sat. Steve's B-day
My parents picked him up and we left
the puppy on the porch and hid. He
was so happy to have his pup, Buck

"Paw"sibilities: Create pockets for additional photos. Make certain to add directions such as "lift" or "open" like the layout shown at left.

CLANCEE

Spring 2000

Remember

Clancee

Come Out & Play

come out and play

Champ is our new little puppy and how cute he was playing with Corey in the yard today! It was so fun to watch them both chasing each other all around the yard and to hear Corey laughing as loud as he could! I know that they will be good buddies for years to come and the laughing and companionship will continue for a very long time!

Patriotic Pup

our Patriotic

Pup

Pet Tails:
In a perfect world, every dog would have a home and every home would have a dog.
    —unknown

Puppy Wardrobe

Puppy Wardrobe

Scrappy

I guess having 2 boys makes me feel like I am missing something. That's why I love to dress my dog!

Puppy Dress Up

KIERSTEN AND MORIAH

I hear lots of giggling coming out of Kiersten's room so I sneak up to see what could be going on. This is what I found! Our 6 year old, very patient, cocker spaniel dressed up in Kiersten's doll clothes! I had to take time to just laugh at the site and how funny Moriah looked! She was just sitting with a pleading look on her face for me to rescue her! So of course I had to go get my camera to be able to show this to Kiersten when she gets older and forgets how she used to torment her dog! They are such good buddies!

P U P P Y

DRESS UP!

Gracie is such a mischievous little puppy! I was unloading the dishwasher one day and had to step away for just a bit and when I returned this is what I found! Of course, I had to run for the camera to catch this little bad puppy on film! She is such a cute little one and it is a good thing since she is always doing such bad things!

GRACIE

G

amusement

Gracie

Woof

Pet Tails: *The dog represents all that is best in man.*
—Etienne Charlet

Cooper

Cooper

Pet Tails: Acquiring a dog may be the only opportunity we have to "choose" a relative.
—Mordecai Siegal

Six Weeks

Abbey's Dog

marissa's new puppy

april 2001

welcome home Rex

"Paw"sibilities: Words are just as important in your layouts as photographs. Tell a story. It will be so interesting to read years later, and it will be such a treasured memory for family members.

Bosom Buddies

darling

Bosom Buddies

Chewy

Meeting Wyatt

PUPPY LOVE

Andrew loves Harley
So much! He had such
fun playing in the yard
with him! He kept
petting him and trying
to kiss him! He held his
leash tight and let him
walk around the
backyard. They were
about the same size!
They looked so cute
together!

Puppy Love ♥ ♥ Puppy Love ♥ ♥ Puppy Love

Puppy Love

Pet Tails: Money will buy a pretty good dog, but it will not buy a wag of its tail.
—Josh Billings

every BOY needs A DOG

I never have been a big pet person. As a child, we were surrounded by cats and dogs. I can remember loving pets back then, but now I simply just don't care for them. I think they are cute, I will pet them, but the thought of having to care for an animal day after day doesn't appeal to me. After your Aunt Marissa got her dog Rex, I saw a glimmer in your eye as you chased him around. You loved that puppy so much. I watched you play with him day after day. You never tired of him being there. You had so much love in your little heart for that dog. After seeing you with him, I knew that every little boy should have a dog. After all, it just wouldn't be fair!

Kyle & Cooper

Summer

Whoever said

You can't

Buy

love

Never

Bought

A

PUPPY

KYLE & COOPER

JUL 5 2004

Puppy Pick Up

PUPPY
PICK
UP

MAY 2004

Woof

C

Woof

calli

March 2005

Love You

love YOU

Pull

Calli at 3 months Old
Calli you were such a sweet puppy. I couldn't
resist that adorable face of yours. You loved to
be outside especially in the snow. You were so
little that we had to keep you on a leash until
such time as you were no longer able to fit
through the fence. I loved to watch you frolic in
the snow even though it was cold my first...

C

mom·ents
cherish
moments
we do not remember days we remember moments
we do not remember days we remember moments
v. to hold dear
mom·ents
[mom·e

Pet Tails:
He is your friend, your partner, your defender, your dog. You are his life, his love, his leader. He will be yours, faithful and true, to the last beat of his heart. You owe it to him to be worthy of such devotion.
—unknown

Slim Poses

"Even overweight, cats instinctively know the cardinal rule: when fat, arrange yourself in slim poses."
- John Weitz

un

couth
ladlylike
inhibited
flattering
comfortable
sophisticated

That Darn Cat

For those of you with a cat as a pet, you probably already have plenty of pictures of the one who runs the house! For some extra fun in your layouts, take photos of all your cat's body parts: ears, paws, whiskers, and little pink nose. Make certian to include bath time, whether it's in the tub or your cat giving himself a bath. The following pages will give you many ideas for your memory books as the designers try to capture this playful pet in their layouts.

Blessed are those who love cats, for they shall never be lonely.
—Unknown

YOU

ME

You and Me together will be
Forever, you'll see
We two can be good company
You and Me
Yes, together, we two
Together, that's you
Forever with me
We'll always be good company

YOU & ME

You & Me

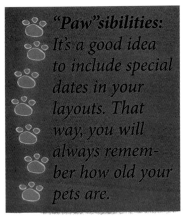

"Paw"sibilities: It's a good idea to include special dates in your layouts. That way, you will always remember how old your pets are.

Tiger

1

happy birthday TIGER

ONE *year old*
August 16, 2004

the 3 Amigos

Frisky *(frisk) adj.* Energetic, lively, and playful.

Snuggle

queen of sheba

the ugly kitten

The Three Amigos

Chance

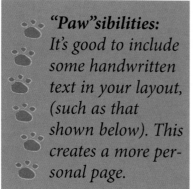

Sophie

s o p h i e

Sophie is a cat that loves to climb trees! On this particular day we couldn't find her so we hunted all over the yard and finally found her up in this tree. She was so cute looking down on us that I had to get my camera to catch her on film.

"Paw"sibilities: It's good to include some handwritten text in your layout, (such as that shown below). This creates a more personal page.

it's WRAP

a sack, tissue paper, packing materials — all are fair game for thomas to curl up and hide in. he attacks the shadows of every object that passes by his make-shift fort. it's a wonder he hasn't suffocated himself for as much time as he spends in his various wraps, hiding from the rest of us.

APRiL 2004

It's a Wrap

GOTCHA

GOTCHA GOTCHA GOTCHA GOTCHA GOTCHA GOTCHA GOTCHA GOTCHA GOTCHA GOT CHA GOTCHA GOTCHA GOT

determination

When Steve came home one day with a kitten, Rebecca realized she had a new friend to follow around. One day, P.J., our kitten, thought he could hide from her by going under the trailer. The problem was that he had a determined, strong-willed little toddler after him, who was also small enough to fit under the trailer. After crawling on her bare knees she finally reached him and showed her delight in her accomplishment.

2003

Determination

Pet Tails: *Dogs come when they are called. Cats take a message and get back to you later.*
—Mary Bly

How Do I Love You?

12

I love the way you love your kitten. You are so gentle with her and never tire of her play. You are quick to help feed and care for her.

how do I ███ you?

let me count the ways

Lester

lester

...ere are many reasons we ...e having the Lester cat in ...r family. He's very soft, so ...s of fun to rub. He has ...e eyes, just like Adelaide. ...'ll sit on your lap for hours and hours. He likes to sleep at the foot of the bed each night. He likes to play with his toys. He doesn't meow very loudly. He loves us just as much as we love him.

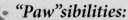

🐾 **"Paw"sibilities:**
🐾 *Type definitions or say-*
🐾 *ings and cut them into*
🐾 *long, narrow strips,*
🐾 *such as these shown at*
🐾 *right. Incorporate these*
🐾 *into your layouts by*
🐾 *going over and under*
🐾 *photographs.*

Jasper & Gracie

Ⓐ stUdy Buddy

EVEN THOUGH HE'S TECHNICALLY MY CAT, A BIRTHDAY PRESENT TO ME, HE MOST DEFINITELY LIKES TO SPEND TIME IN ANDY'S OFFICE IN THE EVENING. ALTHOUGH WE REFER TO HIM AS ANDY'S "STUDY BUDDY," HE USUALLY JUST HINDERS THE PROCESS. HE WANTS ATTENTION, HE LAYS ON ANDY'S TEXT BOOK WHEN HE'S TRYING TO READ — HE WILL TRY ANYTHING! NOT ONLY DO I HAVE AN INTELLIGENT HUSBAND, MY CAT IS SMART TOO!

Study Buddy

Location, Location, Location

LOCATION

locaTIon

LOCATION

IN MY NEXT LIFE, I WANT TO BE A CAT. BESIDE THE
FACT THAT THEY SLEEP MOST OF THE DAY, THEY
WILL CURL UP ANYWHERE AND TAKE ...
TRIP TO MOM AND DAD ...
GO TO BED ONLY TO ...
IN THE BATHROOM SINK ...
TO MOVE EITHER, INSTE ...
LOOK, I GUESS SO WE ...

Pet Tails: *The naming of a cat is a difficult matter. It isn't just one of your holiday games. You may think at first, I'm mad as a hatter. When I tell you a cat must have three different names.*

—*T. S. Elliot*

C A T

Thomas Paulding

The naming of cats is a difficult
matter...not just a game. What he
tells us is every cat must have three
different names. First, his everyday
name - the one the family uses.
Then, he must have a more dignified,
even peculiar name that never belongs
to more than one cat. But most
importantly the secret name that only
the cat himself will know and never
confess.

-T.S. Eliot

Naming a Cat

Magnetic

magnetic: adj. 1.Possessing an extraordinary power or ability to attract. a-|PERSONALITY|

Our kitty, Bunky, is a true Kiddie Magnet! She seems to attract every little kid that enters our home. Little girls seem to be especially fond of her! She isn't particularly thrilled about this since she is 15 years old and these kiddies aren't always the gentlest. She usually hides as quickly as she can! However, sometimes she is spotted before she can escape. She puts up with the attention, but she would much rather be sleeping peacefully in a quiet corner somewhere. After all, isn't that what retirement is suppose to be for, a time to rest?

MIA AND BUNKY

Puff

Look! Look!
See the cat.
See the girl.
Spunky li'l girl hugs
    the cat.
Ouch! Ouch!
That's too tight!
Run, cat, run!
Go! Go!

See the CAT

"Paw"sibilities: Look for vintage images in old books and magazines. The "Dick and Jane" image in the layout at left adds the perfect touch to the page.

See the Cat

(lŭv) [2], to regard with affection **love** (lŭv) [
with affection **love** (lŭv) [2], to regard with a

I LOVE YOU

with affection **love** (lŭv) [2], to regard with a
lŭv'lĭ) [7], beautiful. **lover** (-ẽr), one who

There's Puppy Love........

And then there's......

KITTY LOVE

Pet Tails:
The cat was created when the lion sneezed.
—Arabian Proverb

Kitty Love

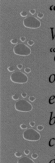

"Paw"sibilities:
While there are many "definition" papers available on the market, you can easily create your own text backgrounds by scanning or cutting up portions of old dictionaries or books.

Best Friends

Thief of Hearts

god made the CAT in order that MAN may have the pleasure of caressing the tiger

Caress the Tiger

THIEF OF HEARTS

Hi Moby. I know you don't speak English but I know you understand what I'm talking about (when you feel like it, that is). You are THE cutest little cat I have ever known. Not only are you drop-dead gorgeous, but you also have the most awesome personality. You're more like a puppy than you are a cat. You steal the show wherever you go! But most of all, you stole my heart. You are so sweet when you come to bed in the middle of the night and try to get under the blankets with me. I reward you by letting you lick the little bit of milk out of my cereal bowl when I'm done because you're so cute how you hang out and wait for me to finish eating it. You're very talkative and you're SO cute when you chirp when the toaster oven dings. You like to lie in the sunshine but because you are totally white, you reflect all the heat and you stay stone cold no matter how hot the sun is. Must be why you love to cuddle! We can never take a picture of you with the flash because the picture just comes out a huge white spot of light. You're too white! Everything reflects off of you. You have these really neat gold eyes which, along with your pink ears and nose, are the only colors on ... your whole body! You absolutely adore getting under blankets. You will do everything you can to work yourself underneath one, and then the purring begins. You only have to TOUCH fleece before you start purring. We'll talk about your bad habits another time.

Pet Tails: One must love a cat on its own terms. —Paul Gray

Fat Cat

F A T C A T

I am not a cat person. I'm positive about that, so what am I doing with not one, but two cats? I think it must be your fault, Adelaide, because you wanted a kitty cat. You begged for a kitty cat. ...and like I've told you many, many times, I am a dog person, not a cat person. I must admit though that this cat has somehow definitely gotten my heart. In fact, I guess you could say I love this 17 pound fur ball...this fat cat named Lester. I loved him so much that I hated for him to be lonely when we were gone, so we got Chester. Lester was supposed to your cat, but he became my constant companion and is never too far away from me. I guess you might say he's turned me into a cat/dog person. That's the story of how we ended up with two cats and the transformation of me. Psst...don't tell anyone I like cats. ☺

lester

Wise

Pet Tails:
Dreaming of a white cat means good luck.
—American Superstition

Cats always seem so very wise,
when staring with their half-closed eyes.
Can they be thinking, "I'll be nice,
and maybe she will feed me twice?"
- bette midler

Duchess

FEATURES FOR WOMEN

FEATURES FOR

Duchess

Duchess

SEVEN

Little Miss Duchess came to our doorstep one hot July evening of 1996 in Lafayette, Indiana. Chris found her outside our duplex when he got home from work. She was dirty and very skinny, except for her tummy, which was very round. She was obviously pregnant. We fed her and took her in right then and there. Later that week, at the veterinarian's office, the doctor confirmed that Duchess was indeed going to have kittens, but assured us that it would be a small litter, only 1 or 2 kittens. Fast-forward to the second week in August. Duchess starting having her "small" litter at around 8:30 am and didn't finish until after 1:00 pm when the SEVENTH kitten was born! Seven tiny little kittens. She was such a wonderful momma to them all. We eventually gave away 5 of the kittens, but kept 2 of them, along with Duchess. She has become such an integral part of our family. She is very sweet and nurturing, and has the softest coat of any cat we've ever known. She definitely has her quirks though. She can't really meow, so her little mouth will open but no sounds come out! Duchess adores Chris and will climb up on his chest anytime he sits still for more than a minute. She is not too fond of Emilee's constant attention but is learning to tolerate her. Duchess is our girly-girl prissy kitty, and we just love her for it!
Photo: June.04

Cats

are like potato chips

PLAY

you can't stop with just

rascal is a bundle of energy. she has a nose for trouble.

—one

Cat or Gargoyle

Cat or Gargoyle

Belle

cat — OR — **GARGOYLE**

Belle-Belle was the first pet I got after moving out of my parents house in 1991. I had never been without a pet before, and was very depressed! So, as a Valentine's Day present my husband (then boyfriend) paid the pet deposit for my apartment and took me to the shelter to choose a kitty. When I saw Belle I knew right away that she was the kitty I wanted! She was so beautiful and friendly! She is such an affectionate kitty cat! She loves to be the center of attention and enjoys being in a lap whenever the opportunity arises. She has been a very faithful friend to me for many years now, and I look forward to many more!

spe·cial (spesh'əl)
or unique 2 exception
for a particular purpo
special person or thin

affectionate

funny faces

Funny Faces

Pet Tails: When moving into a new house, put your cat in through the window instead of the door if you want to keep it there.

Circus Poodles

NOTHING GETS THESE GUYS MOVING LIKE ROTISSERIE CHICKEN! JUST THE SMELL OF IT IS ENOUGH TO SEND THEM INTO A CHIRPING FRENZY, AND THEN THEY DANCE LIKE... *circus poodles?*

circus poodles

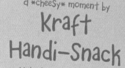

a *cheesy* moment by

Kraft Handi-Snack

Moby is our little feline vacuum cleaner... he will eat anything. At only 1.5 years old he has learned more than his fair share of what human food is good to eat. Processed cheese food? Sure! Bring it on!

Cheesy Moment

Pet Tails: *Cats cannot taste sweets.*

Sweet Tooth

TASTY

YUm

Sweet Tooth

delight (di·lit) 1. to give great pleasure 2. to rejoice, or be highly pleased

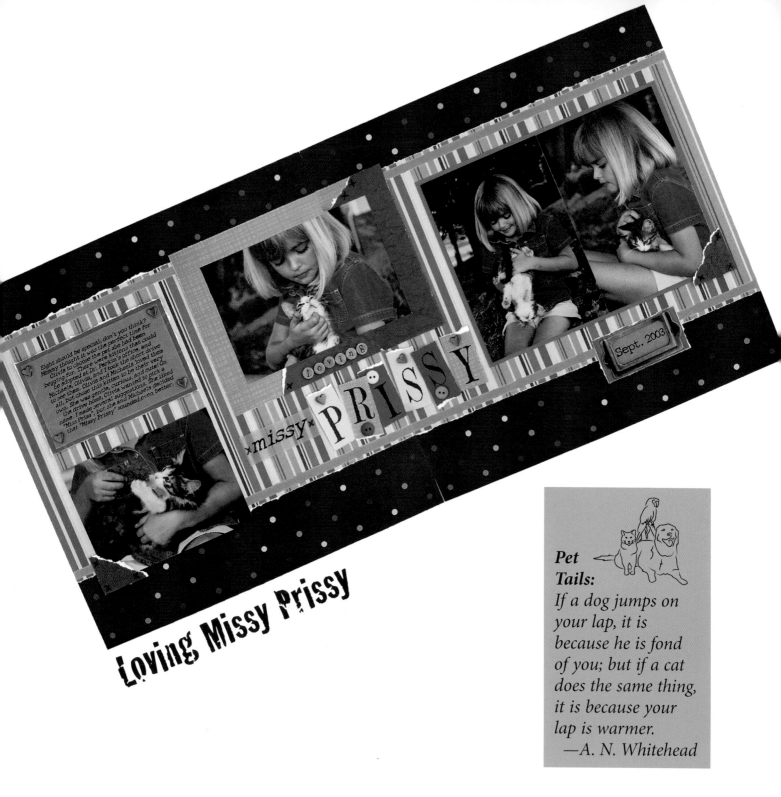

Eight should be special, don't you think? Mommy thought it was the perfect time for Olivia to choose the pet she had been begging for. There were kittens that could be adopted at Dr. Perkin's office, and Michaela, Olivia and I took the short drive to see them. Olivia and Michaela loved them all. She was gentle, curious, and cute! On the drive home, Olivia wanted to pick a name. I made several suggestions. She liked "Miss Prissy," but she and Michaela decided that "Missy Prissy" sounded even better.

loving
missy PRISSY

Sept. 2003

Loving Missy Prissy

Pet Tails: *If a dog jumps on your lap, it is because he is fond of you; but if a cat does the same thing, it is because your lap is warmer.*
—A. N. Whitehead

"Paw"sibilities: Matting photos onto solid paper before placing them onto busy backgrounds help the photos "pop" off the page.

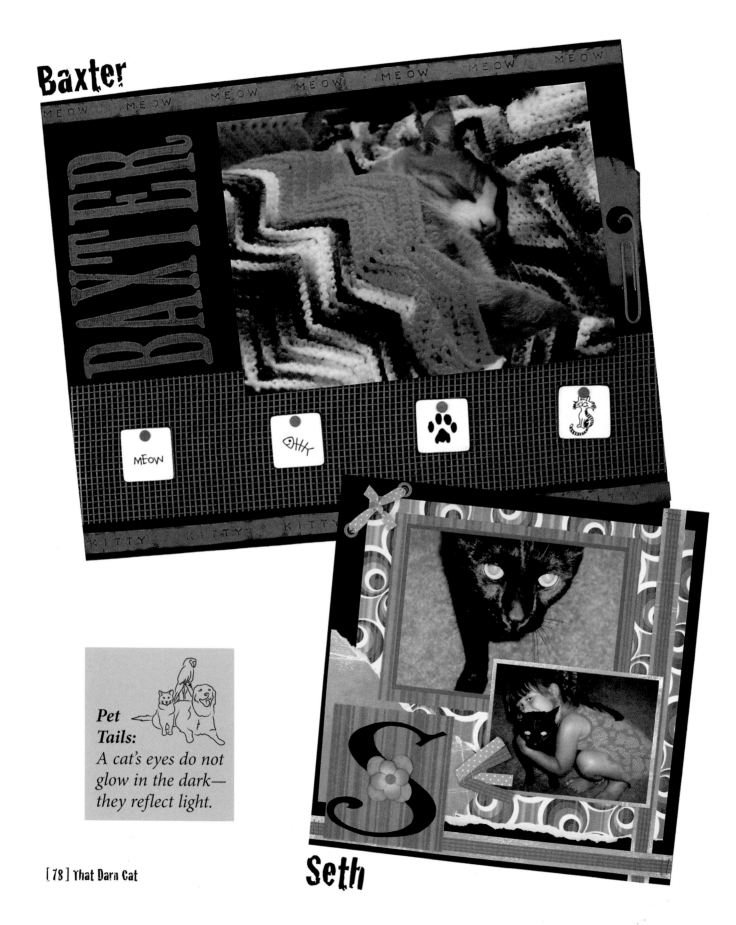

Baxter

BAXTER

MEOW · MEOW · MEOW · MEOW · MEOW

MEOW · MEOW · MEOW

MEOW

KITTY · KITTY · KITTY

Pet Tails: *A cat's eyes do not glow in the dark— they reflect light.*

Seth

ANGER MANAGEMENT

SYMPTOMS.
CHRONICALLY IRRITABLE OR GRUMPY
LOW TOLERANCE FOR FRUSTRATION
UNREASONABLE DEMANDS FOR PERSONAL SPACE

DIXIE AND MOBY
FEB 2004

Anger Management

HEEHAW HEEHAW

DONKEY

Donkey

Old MacDonald's Farm

Maybe your pet is not your typical house pet. A horse or chicken perhaps? Maybe you just have lots of pictures of life on the farm. In this chapter, you will see how our designers incorporated these wonderful animals into their scrapbooks. There are layouts featuring horseback riding, feeding ducks, and even kissing llamas. So pull out your photos and be inspired!

"Any glimpse into the life of an animal quickens our own and makes it so much the larger and better in every way."
- John Muir

> **"Paw"sibilities:** Notice the use of the metal mesh in the layout at right. Trims such as these help to achieve the feel of being at the farm.

Rise 'N Shine

A farm is not a farm until everyone is awakened at the crack of dawn by the crow of a rooster. And Red the Rooster certainly has it down pat.

PRINCE

APPALOOSA

Prince has lived at the buck-nt for about 15 years. after a stint at warrior's state park, Papaw bob brought him back to his farm where the horse has mellowed with age.

Prince

FARM fRieNdS

we love visiting the

PATCH S FARM

OCTOBER 03

Llama Love

Authentic Original

Diana 1996

Llama Love!

absolute delight

100% genuine

Pet Tails: Goats do not actually eat tin cans. They merely nibble on them because the glue on the labels is quite tasty.

Kiss & Hug

KISS AND HUG

For 8 years our family raised llamas. We used them for golf caddies, pack animals, pet therapy for bed-ridden patients, and for educational talks at libraries and a variety of other places. But most of all, we just enjoyed their personalities. Llamas are distinctly individual in their personalities and these 2 particular llamas were tremendously huggy and kissy!

Karee, my gentle, tenderhearted one, loved these two llamas! Emmaus and Sweet Benevolence (Bene) seemed to seek her out for attention. Emmaus was so docile that he would remain in a cushed position and allow Karee to sit beside him and talk. Bene would always come running for kisses and Karee would never disappoint her. Llamas were a cherished, fulfilling way of life for us.

Photos 1997   journaled 8/2004

Pet Tails:
I like pigs. Dogs look up to us. Cats look down on us. Pigs treat us as equals.
-Winston Churchill

THIS Little PIGGY WENT TO SLEEP

This Little Piggy

The fair takes place at the peak of Summer. Sometimes it seems so hard to make the time to go. My hair sticks to the back of my neck, my legs stick to the upholstery of the van's seating. I usually find myself making excuses to skip the annual outing. It's too hot. Too humid. I have a sinus headache. I'm tired & don't feel like it. But in spite of my protests, and maybe a little because of them, I stick a memory card in my front pocket, grab my camera & climb into the van. The reality is, I love the Jasper County fair. It's small. It's small town. Walking onto the fairgrounds is kind of like walking into Cheers. Everybody knows your name. They know your kids' names, what you do for a living and how much you paid for your house. I feel like I'm in the middle of a story. Straight out of Prairie Home Companion. People don't seem to ride the rides a lot. And fewer play the carnival games. But everyone hits the United Methodist food stand and buys the plant entries.

See the Wonder

This was Kierstens first time riding a horse and it was quite the experience for her. We can't say that she really liked it as she cried for it to stop, but at least she tried and that is what really counts. She really liked petting the horse and getting to know her but when the horse started to walk Kiersten didn't like how it moved and it scared her a little bit. But once she was off the horse she went right up to pet her again so that was good. She is our brave little girl! One day she will ride again!

see the wonder...

June

Ducks

Pet Tails: Horses are measured in "hands." A hand is 4". Anything under 14 hands is considered a pony.

DUCKS

One of the highlights of our vacation was visiting Steves brother on their farm in New York. Kiersten loved seeing all the different animals and wanted to hold them all. They had just had some baby ducks born and we went down to the pond for Kiersten to see them and hopefully be able to feed them. They were a little shy but with much coaxing and being very still we got to feed them and Mike was even able to get one for Kiersten to see up close. She was amazed at how big the feet were and how fuzzy it was! It was such a fun experience for all of us to have!

Pet Tails: *The average cow drinks 30 gallons of water and eats 95 pounds of feed per day.*

Hi, Little Goat

Hi, little goat

Fall

Baby Calf

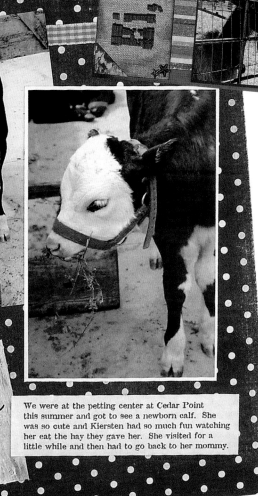

Calf

We were at the petting center at Cedar Point this summer and got to see a newborn calf. She was so cute and Kiersten had so much fun watching her eat the hay they gave her. She visited for a little while and then had to go back to her mommy.

Moo Cow

Dream Pony

Smile Goat

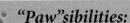
"Paw"sibilities:
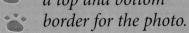
In the layout above, the zipper was opened into two pieces and used as a top and bottom border for the photo.

Quarter

Oh how I wish I would have taken a picture of quarter the day we got him. He got his name honestly, he was actually the size of a quarter when we got him. He arrived by 2 day mail in a box with the words, "fragile, live harmless reptile" on the outside. When the man handed the box to me he said, "Is there really a live harmless reptile in there?" Sure enough. Tucked inside a big mac type container with tissue all around him was this tiny turtle the size of a quarter. Branden took great care setting up just the right habitat for him. And he has thrived. He has grown so much that we can't even believe that he is the same turtle.

Photos taken Summer 2004

Quarter

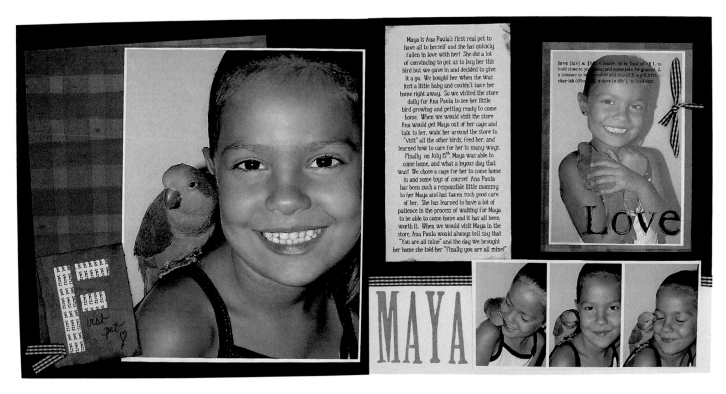

Critters, Creatures & Crawlers

Do you have an unusual pet, a snake or frog, a hamster or bunny? Even fish can be included in your layouts! These animals are as much a part of your family as a dog or cat. In the following chapter, you will find inspirational layouts for all of these creatures, from bunnies to snakes; there is even a pet snail! You will be excited to find new ways to include these smaller animals in your family albums.

> " Behold the turtle. He makes progress only when
> he sticks his neck out."
>
> -James Bryant Conant

Hamster Head

Lily's New Pet

Lily's New PET

HAMSTER HEAD

LILY AND HER PET HAMSTER STUART LOVE GOOFING OFF TOGETHER! OF COURSE DADDY COULDN'T RESIST PUTTING HIM ON HER HEAD. SHE DID NOT MIND. SHE KEPT LOOKING UP AT HIM AND GIGGLING!

2004

LOVE

Pet Tails:
All pet hamsters are descended from a single female wild golden hamster found with a litter of 12 young in Syria in 1930.

"Paw"sibilities: In the layout at left, game tiles were used to title the page.

Beauty

♥ beauty ♥ beauty ♥ beauty

Precious   SILLY   SNUGGLE

with love

B U N N Y
L O V E

Bunny Love

Beauty

GIRL

beauty may have charm and good looks, but sometimes she's a little terror. yet when i see that cute little pink nose, my heart just melts. she's my baby. ♥

Bunny Boy

OUR CUTE SWEET

BUNNY BOY

WE LOVE

New Friend

New

Fascinating

FRIEND

Sierra the girl

grassy the snail

Pet Tails:
Rabbits don't like it when you rearrange their cages when you clean. They are creatures of habit, and when they get something just right, they like to keep it that way.

Zippy the Fish

ZIPPY ☆ THE ☆ FISH

No one can tell me that fish don't have personalities. I know different! Zippy loves me! When I get home from work, he zips around his fishbowl like he's excited to see me. Of course, I'm sure it's just because he's hungry, but I like to think differently. He's fast, too. In fact, I think he's the fastest fish in the East!

Stuart

STUaRt

We wanted a small pet for lily. We knew right away that a hamster was the best one for us! The minute she saw him she wanted to name him stuart from the movie stuart little. We got him a cool cage with tunnels and a wheel and Stuart was home sweet home!

our — pet — hamster

Pet Tails:
Goldfish lose their color if left in dim light, or if they are placed in a running water source like a stream.

Bingo

LOVING
SILLY
FUN
FUZZY
FRIEND
PLAYFUL

BINGO
THE GUINEA PIG

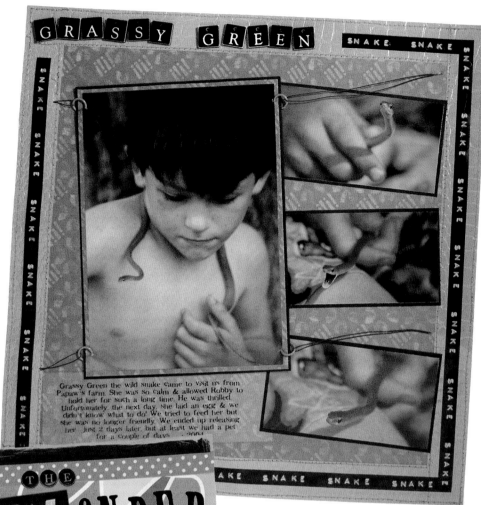

GRASSY GREEN

SNAKE SNAKE SNAKE

SNAKE

Grassy Green the wild snake came to visit us from Papaw's farm. She was so calm & allowed Robby to hold her for such a long time. He was thrilled. Unfortunately, the next day, she laid an egg & we didn't know what to do! We tried to feed her but she was no longer friendly. We ended up releasing her just 2 days later, but at least we had a pet for a couple of days ... 2004

SNAKE SNAKE SNAKE SNAKE

The Wonder

THE

WONDER
of it all

wonderful: adj. 1.Exciting wonder, 2.Marvelous, astonishing. 3.Unusually good. 4.A sight to behold. (ADMIRABLE!)

PULL

relax

R

unwind

2004

Grassy Green

Allergy Free Al

Pet Tails: There are 2,600 different species of frogs. They live on every continent except Antarctica.

Discover

Molly & Kenny

Kissing Frogs

This is not my daughter! Where is that amphibian phobia that she inherited from me? Instead of fear-- Berea has hope. Hope that the next one will be her prince!

kissing frogs

ONE SIZE FITS ALL
50% Laughter
40% Loyalty
10% Love

Hand Wash Warm

PALS BUDDIES FRIENDS

friend

USE Soap!

Daisy

Macaw

DAISY

Daisy was the

MAY

2003

love

Turtle crazy

discover

Turtle Crazy

Franklin

FRANKLIN THE FERRET

Franklin has been a part of our family for 2 years now and we love him so much! He loves to wander around the house to see what kind of place he can hide. One of his favorite places to hide is in between the books on the bookshelf! We always find him in the most interesting places, silly little Franklin!

Pet Tails: The pet ferret was domesticated 500 years before the house cat.

Found Turtle

Pet Tails: Iguanas can stay under water for 28 minutes.

Iggy

iggy the iguana soaks up the sun

iggy

Unexpected Beauty

unexpected *beauty*

coils

I was not thrilled when Branden got a snake. Yes, I gave my permission but not with joy in my heart. I was trying to be a "nice mother" and let the boy have a pet...but why oh why did it have to be a snake? Never the less I gave my permission with the caution that "if that snake ever escapes...he's DEAD!" But something has happened over time. I worry about the snake. I ask Branden if he's fed him lately. I check his water. I talk to him!

And I've derived what a truly beautiful creature he is. The colors on his body are so vibrant and so different from anything else I've seen. Dare it, I think, I like him. That I not to say that I would want him slithering freely in my house but I have to admit that I'm not afraid to have him here. I have found in him an unexpected beauty.

Photos taken Summer 2004

Country Girl

COUNTRY
girls
BUD

raccoon

Hannah fell in love fast with these orphaned baby raccoons, that her aunt and uncle rescued, her dad had to practically pry them out of her little arms she wanted to carry them everywhere! she took very good care of them feeding and cleaning their cage. She did have a little help after all she is only three. But being a country girl and living on a farm I am sure, Hannah will help all kinds of different animals while she is growing up.

"Paw"sibilties:
If you don't have a lot of space on your page for journaling, create a small book as shown above. Attach the pages with small hinges on one side.

Carter's Zoo

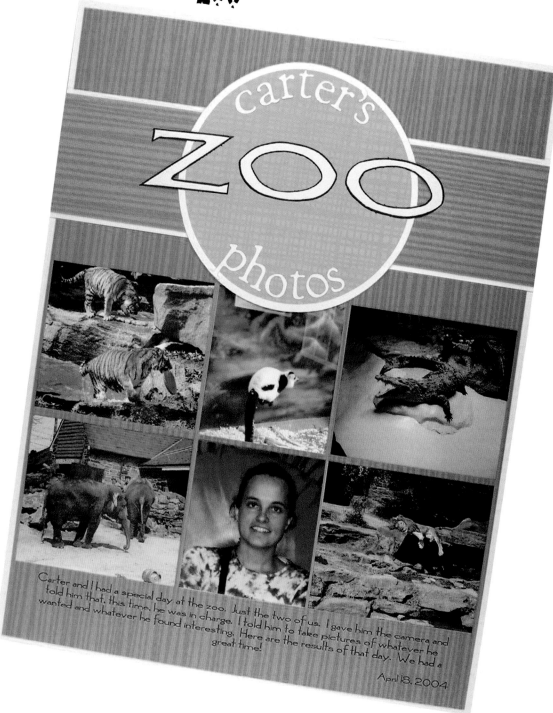

Carter and I had a special day at the zoo. Just the two of us. I gave him the camera and told him that, this time, he was in charge. I told him to take pictures of whatever he wanted and whatever he found interesting. Here are the results of that day. We had a great time!

April 18, 2004

Rhino or Dino?

Carter got so excited as we walked up to the Rhinocerous area of the Philadelphia zoo. The Rhino was unusually active and even came right down by the railing to bathe in the water for a bit. It was incredible to watch him this closely. This Rhino looked so old...I'm not sure if that's the right word for it but he certainly seems to have seen better days. His horn looks downright sad and that skin...prehistoric is about the only way to describe it. It was only after we watched him for awhile that we realized the cause for Carter's excitement. "I can't believe our zoo has a real dinosaur! Is that a real dinosaur?" His excitement was slightly dampened as we explained that we were looking at a "rhino" not a "dino". But we all agreed that this is one magnificent animal!

At the zoo At the zoo At the zoo At the zoo At the zoo At the zoo At the zoo At the zoo At the zoo At the zoo At the zoo At the zoo At the zoo At the zoo At the zoo At the zo

AUGUST 2003

Zoo Discovery

If you don't have pets, but your favorite family outing is a day at the zoo, this chapter is for you. You can find every kind of animal doing all kinds of things at the zoo. Capture animals resting, playing, eating, or bathing, all within a natural-looking habitat. So next time you go to the zoo, be certian to take your camera; because our designers have shown you a variety of fun ways to scrapbook these memories.

The zoo is a place for animals to study the behavior of human beings.
-Author unknown

MY DREAM PET

I'VE ALWAYS BEEN FASCINATED WITH PARROTS. THEIR COLORS, STRENGTH, AND INTELLIGENCE KEEP ME IN AWE. OWNING ONE WOULD BE A DREAM COME TRUE.

2004

SEA WORLD

CALIFORNIA

BUMP ON A LOG

Sea World

"Paw"sibilities: When taking photos of animals, zoom in and get as close as possible. This will make for better scrapbook pages.

2 Sleepy Pandas

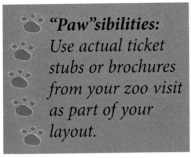

"Paw"sibilities: Use actual ticket stubs or brochures from your zoo visit as part of your layout.

The Zoo

Pet Tails: The largest zoo animals are elephants. The males can weigh between 10,000 and 12,000 pounds.

Elephants

Brrr...

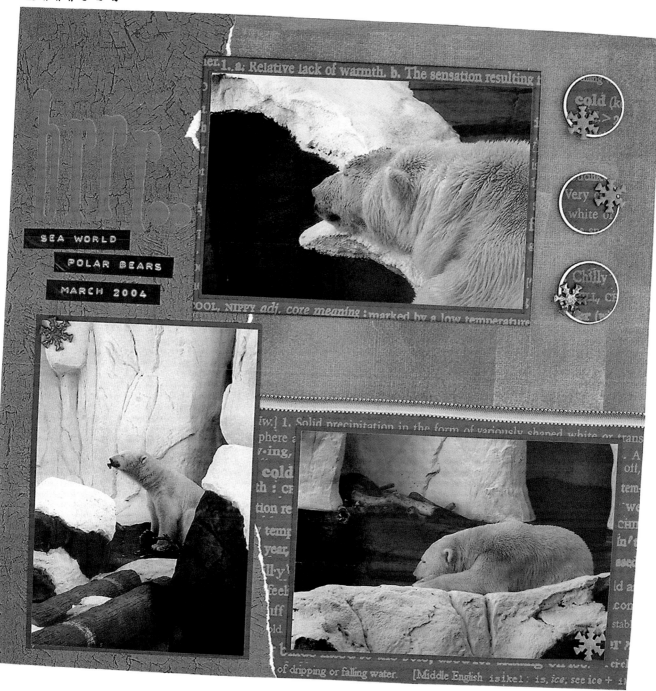

SEA WORLD
POLAR BEARS
MARCH 2004

Tiger Cubs

There are tiger cubs at the Philadelphia Zoo!!! We didn't even know this when we went to the zoo but there they were. They aren't tiny but they are so cute! I know cute doesn't seem like the right word for a tiger but these tigers act just like kittens. They were playing constantly...pouncing, running, jumping on the mother tiger (and boy did she look annoyed), and playing with a green bucket lid as if it were a Frisbee. They were even practicing their stalking on their mother. It was so much fun to watch. We could have stayed there all afternoon watching their hijinx, but eventually the draw of the reptile house called and we were off...

April 2004

Tiger Cubs

SAN DIEGO ZOO

JunE

2004

mys-ter-y (mis'te re, -tre), n., pl. -teries. Something secret or impossible to understand. Something arousing curiosity through its obscure nature.

ABOUT THE ORANGUTAN:

The orangutan, with its reddish-brown, shaggy hair, has a strong, heavily built body, and is the second-largest primate. The arms are long and powerful and reach to the ankles when the animal stands erect; there is a small thumb on each broad hand that is opposable to the first digit. The orangutan's legs are relatively short and weaker than the arms. Males are much larger and heavier than females and are also identified by the cheek flaps that surround the face of the mature adult. Orangutans live alone, in pairs or in small family groups and are active in the daytime at all levels of the trees. They walk along large branches on all fours or erect and sometimes swing by their hands from branch to branch. On the ground, they walk on all fours or stand erect. Fruit is their staple diet, but they also feed on leaves, seeds, young birds and eggs. The orangutan sleeps in the trees in a platform nest made of sticks; it may make a new nest every night.

"Paw"sibilites:
Postage stamps make great additions to your page. Try to find stamps that are related to the page. In this case, the stamps could be from the countries where orangutans are found.

Project Materials & Index

Page 1 Meow

Designer Elizabeth Ruuska

Brad (Boxer)
Cardstock (Club Scrap, Paper Loft)
Computer Font (Trubble)
Domino
Faux Postage (100 Proof Press)
Ink (Ranger Inc., Staz On, Tsukineko)
Jump Ring
Kitten Stamp (Bizzaro)
Letter Stamps (PSX)
Photo Turn (7gypsies)
Safety Pin (Making Memories)
Snaps

Pages 2-3 Puppy in Love

Designer Renee Villalobos-Campa

Embroidery Floss (DMC)
Letter Buttons (Junkitz)
Letter Stickers (Artic Frog)
Machine Stitching
Patterned Paper (Artic Frog)

Page 4 For the Birds

Designer Vanessa Hudson

Cardstock (Bazzill)
Diecuts (KI Memories)
Fiber (Making Memories)
Ink (Color Box)
Patterned Paper (KI Memories)
Stamps (Stamp Craft)
Vellum (Bazzill)

Page 6 Dig In

Designer Tonya Borrosch

Cardstock (Bazzill)
Fonts (Hootie, Jump Start)
Label Maker (Dymo)
Machine Stitching
Patterned Paper (Arctic Frog)

Page 7 My Pride, My Joy

Designer Tonya Borrosch

Letter Stickers (David Walker)
Magenta Patterned Papers (Making
    Memories)

Bookplate (Making Memories)
Ink (Making Memories)
Transparencies (Magic Scraps)
Washers (Making Memories)
Stamp (Hero Arts Script)
Mini Brads (2 Peas in a Bucket)

Page 8 Louie and Mickie

Designer Diana Furey

Brads (Making Memories)
Cardstock (Bazzill)
Computer Font (Blue Highway
    Condensed)
Envelopes (Nostalgiques)
Folio Closure (Colorbok)
Hemp
Key
Machine Stitching
Patterned Papers (Chatterbox)
Ribbon
Rub-ons (Making Memories)
Tassel
Twill (7gypsies)
Wooden Tiles (7gypsies)

Page 9 Rescued

Designer Diana Furey

Brads (Joanne's)
Cardstock (Bazzill)
Craft Paint (Golden)
Hinges (Making Memories)
Label Holder (Making Memories)
Leather Flowers (Making Memories)
Mesh Eyelets (Making Memories)
Page Marker (Sweetwater)
Patterned Papers (Chatterbox)
Poetry Dog Tags
Ribbon (Li'l Davis)
Stamps (Ma Vinci)
Transparency (Creative Imaginations)
Wood Letters (Li'l Davis)

Page 10 Blue-eyed Relay

Designer Shannon Taylor

Adhesive (Therm-O-Web)
Burlap
Cardstock
Embroidery Floss (DMC)
Eye Charm

Ink (Stampin' Up)
Letter Rub-ons (Scrapworks)
Machine Stitching
Patterned Papers (Rusty Pickle)
Ribbon (Offray)
Tape (Therm-O-Tape)

Page 11 Cherish

Designer Tonya Borrosch

Beads
Bookplate (2 Peas in a Bucket)
Brads (2 Peas in a Bucket)
Cardstock
Computer Font (Times New Roman)
Eyelets (Making Memories)
Frame (This and That)
Ink (Making Memories)
Machine Stitching
Patterned Papers (Chatterbox)
Ribbon (Offray)
Word Stickers (Bo-Bunny)

Page 11 Play Time

Designer Candace Leonard

Brads (Making Memories)
Cardstock
Computer Font (Adler)
Craft Paint (Making Memories)
Papers (Basic Grey)
Rub-ons (Making Memories)
Stamps (Making Memories)
Stickers (Creative Imaginations)
Tags (Basic Grey)

Page 11 Pet Peeves

Designer Candace Leonard

Bottle Caps (Li'l Davis)
Computer Font (Tasklist from
    2 Peas in a Bucket)
Craft Paint (Making Memories)
Date Stamp (Making Memories)
Foam Stamps (Making Memories)
Jump Rings (Junkitz)
Papers (Li'l Davis)
Ribbon (May Arts)
Staples
Tag (Avery)
Tile (Junkitz)

Page 12 Backyard Adventure

Designer Janice Lund

Cardstock (Bazzill)
Letter Stickers (Sticker Studio)
Patterned Papers (Daisy D's)
Ribbon (May Arts)
Zipper Pull (Junkitz)

Page 12 Always Together

Designer Renee Villalobos-Campa

Buttons
Cardstock
Embroidery Floss (DMC)
Letter Buttons (Junkitz)
Patterned Papers

Page 12 Puppy Promenade

Designer Janice Lund

Cardstock (Bazzill)
Computer Font (39 Smooth)
Letters (QuicKutz)
Metal-Rimmed Tag (Making
    Memories)
Patterned Papers (Art Warehouse,
    Creative Imaginations)
Ribbon (May Arts)
Rickrack (Wrights)
Staples (Making Memories)
Transparency (HammerHill)

Page 13 Dad's Li'l Buddy

Designer Diana Furey

Brads (Boxer)
Cardstock (Bazzill)
Flower
Hinges (Making Memories)
Label Holder (Making Memories)
Letter Charms (Making Memories)
Papers (Carolee's Creations,
    Mustard Moon)
Ribbon (Li'l Davis, Offray)
Rub-ons (Doodlebug)
Safety Pins (Making Memories)
Synonym Tab (Autumn Leaves)
Wooden Letters (Li'l Davis)

Page 14 Best of Buddies

Designer Diana Furey

Brads (Boxer)
Cardstock (Bazzill)
Clay Phrases (Li'l Davis)
Copper Letters (Making Memories)

Office Envelopes (Autumn Leaves)
Patterned Papers (Bo-Bunny,
Chatterbox)
Ribbon (Darice)
Watch Face (Jest Charming)

Page 14 Bailey & Jim

Designer Diana Furey

Brads (Joanne's)
Buttons (Junkitz)
Cardstock (Memories Complete)
Clip (Making Memories)
Elastic Holder (7gypsies)
File Folder (Autumn Leaves)
Ink (Ranger Inc.)
Letter Stickers (Creative Imaginations)
Papers (Chatterbox)
Ribbon (May Arts)
Tag
Twill Letters (Carolee's)
Twill Ribbon (7gypsies)
Twill Sayings (AMM)
Wood Flowers (Li'l Davis)
Word Phrases (Li'l Davis)

Page 14 Dog Dictionary

Designer Melanie Bauer

Brad (Making Memories)
Cardstock (Chatterbox)
Label Maker (Dymo)
Letter (Making Memories)
Metal Tag (MakingMemories)
Patterned Papers (Chatterbox)
Pen (EK Success)
Ribbon (Offray)
Stickers (Mrs. Grossman's,
    Stickopotamus)

Page 15 A Dog's Heart

Designer Diana Furey

Brads (Joanne's)
Buttons (Jesse James)
Cardstock (Bazzill)
Label Holder (Making Memories)
Machine Stitching
Patterned Papers (KI Memories)

Ribbon (Li'l Davis, May Arts, Offray)
Ribbon Charm (Making Memories)
Rub-ons (Doodlebug)
Transparency
Wooden Flowers (Li'l Davis)

Page 16 Faithful Friendship

Designer Janet Hopkins

Brad (Making Memories)
Brads
Cardstocks (Bazzill)
Computer Font (Adler)
Foam Stamps (Making Memories)
Hinges (Making Memories)
Paint (Making Memories)
Paper Clip (7gypsies)
Patterned Papers (Chatterbox)
Ribbon (Offray)
Rub-ons (C-Thru Ruler)
Stencil
Transparency

Page 17 Calli

Designer Janine Vanderhorst

Buckle
Buttons (SEI)
Cardboard Paper (Pebbles)
Label Maker (Dymo)
Machine Stitching
Nails (Chatterbox)
Patterned Papers (American Crafts)
Photo Turns (7gypsies)
Ribbon (Bobbin Brown, May Arts)
Rub-ons (Making Memories)

Page 17 Best Friend

Designer Janice Lund

Buttons (Junkitz)
Cardstock (Chatterbox)
Computer Font (Tubby from
    2 Peas in a Bucket)
Index Tabs (7gypsies)
Jump Rings (Junkitz)
Letter Stickers (Deluxe Designs,
    Pebbles, Creative Imaginations)
Machine Stitching
Patterned Papers (Chatterbox)
Ribbon (May Arts)
Staples (Making Memories)
Stencils (Autumn Leaves)
Synonym Tabs (Autumn Leaves)
Transparency (HammerHill)
Zipper Pull (Junkitz)

Page 17 We Are Family

Designer Sharon Geibig

Brads (Making Memories)
Cardstock (Bazzill)
Craft Paint (Making Memories)
Dictionary Strip (Making Memories)
Foam Stamps (Making Memories)
Patterned Papers (Making Memories)
Rub-ons (Autumn Leaves)

Page 18 My Dog

Designer Diana Furey

Brads (Joanne's)
Cardstock (Bazzill)
Computer Font (Well Behaved from
    2 Peas in a Bucket)
Craft Paint (Plaid)
Embroidery Floss (DMC)
Flowers (Making Memories)
Ink (Chalk-a-Lots)
Machine Stitching
Mini Tags (Making Memories)
Page Marker (Sweet Water)
Patterned Papers (Chatterbox,
    Mustard Moon)
Phrase Charm (Making Memories)
Ribbon (Darice)
Stamp (Making Memories)
Transparency
Word Pebble (Li'l Davis)
Word Washers (Making Memories)

Page 18 Buddies

Designer Diana Furey

Brads (Boxer, Joanne's)
Cardstock (Bazzill)
Flowers (Making Memories)
Hinges (Making Memories)
Ink (Chalk-a-lots)
Label Holder (Making Memories)
Machine Stitching
Patterned Papers (Chatterbox,
    Leisure Arts)
Ribbon (Morex Corp.)
Stamps (Making Memories)

Page 18 Our Sweet Girl

Designer Candace Leonard

Brads (Making Memories)
Craft Paint (Making Memories)
Flowers (Making Memories)
Ink (Ranger Inc.)

Patterned Papers (SEI)
Ribbon
Rub-ons (Craf-T Products)
Stamps (Making Memories)
Tiles (Junkitz)

Page 19 Calli's Album

Designer Janine Vanderhorst

Cardstock (Bazzill, Chatterbox)
Craft Paint
Ink (Ranger Inc.)
Jump Rings (Junkitz)
Letter Stickers (Sonnets)
Machine Stitching
Metal Letter (Making Memories)
Molding Strips (Chatterbox)
Papers (Chatterbox)
Ribbon (May Arts)
Silk Flower
Tag (Chatterbox)
Zipper Pulls (Junkitz)

Page 20 Cool in the Pool

Designer Stacey Panassidi

Cardstock (KI Memories)
Jump Rings (Junkitz)
Letter Stickers (KI Memories)
Patterned Papers (KI Memories)
Tags (KI Memories)

Page 21 Summer Splash

Designer Janine Vanderhorst

Cardstock (Bazzill)
Jump Ring (Junkitz)
Letter Buttons (Junkitz)
Letter Sticker (American Crafts)
License Plates (Junkitz)

Page 21 D Is for Dog

Designer Tonya Borrosch

Bottle Caps (Li'l Davis)
Cardstock (Bazzill)
Computer Fonts (Texas Hero and
    Stamp Act from Scrap Village,
    Times New Roman)
Conchas (Scrapworks)
Flowers (JoLee's)
Patterned Papers (American Crafts)
Poetry Dog Tag
Word Tags (Scrapworks)

Page 22 Love You to Pieces

Designer Heather Preckel

Buttons (Junkitz)
Cardstock
Cardstock Letters (Foofala)
Patterned Papers (Daisy D's)
Pen (EK Success)
Puzzle Pieces (Li'l Davis)
Trim (Me and My Big Ideas)

Page 22 Hippie Chick

Designer Stacy Yoder

Ink (Stampin' Up)
Letter Stamps (PSX)
Patterned Papers (SEI)
Ribbon (SEI)
Rub-ons (SEI)
Sticker Word (Creative Imaginations)
Stickers (Creative Imaginations SEI)
Tags (SEI)

Page 22 Newborn Love

Designer Stacey Panassidi

Brads (Happy Hammer)
Cardstock
Craft Paint
Letter Buttons (EK Success)
Machine Stitching
Patterned Papers (Chatterbox)
Rub-on (Making Memories)

Page 23 Hula Pup

Designer Vanessa Hudson

Buttons (Junkitz)
Cardstock (Bazzill)
Computer Font (Proud Pa Pa from
    2 Peas in a Bucket)
Flowers (Making Memories)
Grass Skirt Pieces
Papers (Paper Adventures)

Page 24 Canine Companion

Designer Sharon Geibig

Brads (Making Memories)
Cardstock (Bazzill)
Date Stamp (Making Memories)
Label Holders (Making Memories)
Patterned Papers (Chatterbox,
    KI Memories)
Rub-ons (Making Memories)
Transparency (Artistic Expressions)

Pages 3i Innocent

Designer Erika Follansbee

Computer Font (Last Words)
Fiber (Awesome Albums)
Papers (Carolee's Creations, Chatterbox)
Sticker (Creative Imaginations)

Page 32 Kitty in a Box

Designer Melanie Bauer

Cardstock (Bazzill)
Patterned Papers (KI Memories)
Pen (EK Success)
Ribbon (Offray)
Slide Holder (Boxer)
Stickers (Creative Imaginations, Doodlebug, MAMBI)

Page 32 Gray Kitty

Designer Polly McMillan

Bottle Cap (Li'l Davis)
Buttons (Making Memories)
Flower Punch (EK Success)
Letter Tool (QuicKutz)
Library Card
Papers (Laura Ashley)
Ribbon (Queen & Co.)
Silk Flower
Stamps (PSX)
Tags (7gypsies)

Page 32 Feline Friend

Designer Stacy Yoder

Eyelets (Making Memories)
Jumping Rings (Junkitz)
Letter Button (Junkitz)
Letter Stickers (KI Memories)
Patterned Papers (KI Memories)
Ribbon (May Arts)
Transparency (Artistic Expressions)

Page 32 How Do I Love You?

Angelia Wigginton

Buttons (Junkitz)
Cardstock
Computer Font (Hot Chocolate from 2 Peas in a Bucket)
Heart Snaps (Making Memories)
Metal Bookplate (Making Memories)
Metal Letters (Making Memories)
Patterned Papers (Chatterbox)
Round Snaps (Making Memories)

Page 33 Keisha & Princess

Designer Heather Preckel

Cardstock
Expression Sticker (Wordsworth)
Label Maker (Dymo)
Patterned Papers (EK Success, Rusty Pickle)
Ribbon (Li'l Davis)
Wood Flowers (Li'l Davis)

Page 34 Ashlee & Amos

Designer Amy O'Neil

Bead Letter Stickers (Bo-Bunny)
Cardstock (Bazzill)
Craft Paint
Flower Foam Stamp (Making Memories)
Heart Brad
Patterned Papers (Bo-Bunny, Chatterbox)
Stencil Tag
Tile License Plate (Junkitz)

Page 34 Kisses

Designer Elizabeth Ruuska

Buttons (Junkitz)
Cardstock (Bazzill, Close to My Heart, Club Scrap)
Ink (ColorBok Staz On)

Laminate Chips (Pezzo)
Letter Stamps (Ma Vinci, PSX)
Ribbon (Offray)
Tag (Macco)
Vellum Sticker (Mrs. Grossman's)
Zipper (Junkitz)

Page 35 Peek-a-Boo Kittens

Designer Stacy Yoder

CardStock (SEI)
Epoxy Letter (Creative Imaginations)
Letter Stickers (SEI)
Patterned Papes (SEI)
Ribbon
Tag (SEI)

Page 35 Newborn Kittens

Designer Stacy Yoder

Flowers (Savvy Stamps)
Ink (Stampin' Up)
Letter Buttons (Junkitz)
Letter Stamps (PSX)
Letter Stencil (Autumn Leaves)
Machine Stitching
Patterned Papers (Chatterbox)
Rub-ons (Junkitz)

Page 36 Couch Kitty

Designer Melanie Bauer

Cardstock (Bazzill)
Clip (Making Memories)
Embroidery Floss
Letter Charm (Making Memories)
Patterned Papers (7gypsies, Chatterbox, KI Memories)
Pen (EK Success)
Stamps (Hero Arts, PSX)
Stickers (Doodlebug)
Tag (Making Memories)

Page 36 Three Little Kittens

Designer Elizabeth Ruuska

Date Stamps (Making Memories)
Frame (Decorative Details, Nunn Design)
Ink (Staz On, Ranger Inc.)
Machine Stitching
Paper Clips (7gypsies)
Patterned Papers (7gypsies, K&Co.)
Photo Turn (Making Memories)
Ribbon
Stickers (Nostalgiques, Shotz, Sticko)

Page 37 Patience

Designer Elizabeth Ruuska

Brads (Making Memories)
Cardstock (Bazzill)
Flowers
Ink (Colorbok, Ranger Inc., Vintage Photo, Versamagic)
Letters (Foofala)
Patterned Papers (Design Originals)

Page 37 Cap'n Jack Sparrow

Designer Elizabeth Ruuska

Cardstock (Bazzill)
Dimensional Letters (K&Co.)
Label Maker (Dymo)
Letter Stickers (Me and My Big Ideas)
Letter Tool (QuicKutz)
Letters (USArtquest Mica)
Paper Clip (K&Co.)
Patterned Papers (K&Co., Karen Foster)
Pin Backs
Rub-ons (Li'l Davis)
Tag (7gypsies)

Page 38 Cat Eyes

Designer Heather Preckel

Patterned Papers (Carolee's)
Ribbon (Li'l Davis)
Staples
Token (EK Success)

Page 39 Kitty Fishing

Designer Melanie Bauer

Button
Cardstock (Chatterbox)
Fluid Chalk Ink (Colorbok)
Machine Stitching
Patterned Papers (Chatterbox, KI Memories, Rusty Pickle)
Pen (EK Success)
Ribbon (Offray)
Stamps (Ma Vinci)
Token (Doodlebug)

Page 39 Here Kitty

Designer Diana Furey

Cardstock (Bazzill)
Clay Phrase (Li'l Davis)
Computer Font (CK Newsprint)
Letter Tokens (Scrapworks)
Papers (American Crafts, Bo-Bunny, Doodlebug)

Ribbon (Offray)
Rub-ons (Making Memories)
Word Plate (Scrapworks)

Page 40 Ivy & Blythe

Designer Elizabeth Ruuska

Cardstock (Butcher Block)
Clock Stamp (Magenta)
Handmade Diamond Cork Stamp
Leather Frames (Making Memories)
Letter Stamps (PSX)
Letter Tool (QuicKutz)
Letters (Butcher Block)
Patterned Papers (Deja Views)
Ribbon (Making Memories)
Sunflower (Making Memories)
Tag (Butcher Block)

Page 40 Kitty Gingivitis

Designer Melanie Bauer

Cardstock (Bazzill)
Clip (Boxer)
Computer Font (Typo from 2 Peas in a Bucket)
Patterned Papers (KI Memories)
Pen (EK Success)
Snaps (Making Memories)

Page 41 Christmas Cutie

Designer Erika Follansbee

Bottle Cap (Li'l Davis Designs)
Cardstock
Computer Font (Virginia)

Page 41 Kitty Christmas

Designer Melanie Bauer

Bookplate (Making Memories)
Cardstock (Chatterbox)
Patterned Papers (Jennifer Collection, Rusty Pickle)
Pen (EK Success)
Stickers (Creative Imaginations, MAMBI, Stickopotamus)
Vellum (Chatterbox)

Page 42 One, Two Kitty

Designer Annette Lauts

Brads (Making Memories)
Cardstock (Pebbles)
Computer Font (CK Journaling)
Label Maker (Dyno)
Letter Diecuts (QuickKutz)

Metal Letter (Scrapworks)
Number Stencil (Li'l Davis)
Patterned Paper (SEI)
Ribbon

Page 43 Sable

Designer Diana Furey

Bottle Cap (Li'l Davis Designs)
Brads (Boxer)
Cardstock (Bazzil Basic)
Computer Font (CK Fresh)
Craft Paint (Plaid)
Letter Charms (Making Memories)
Letter Stickers (Art Warehouse)
Metal Letters (Junkitz)
Mini Folder (Nostalgiques)
Paper (Doodlebug, Karen Foster)
Ribbon (May Arts, Li'l Davis Designs)
Shaped Clip (Making Memories)
Stencil (Headlines)
Word Charm (All My Memories)
Word Stickers (Art Warehouse)

Page 43 I Scrapped the Cat

Designer Shannon Taylor

Brads (Doodlebug Designs)
Buckle (Junkitz)
Cardstock (Rusty Pickle)
Double Plays (Junkitz)
Fabric (Junkitz)
Ink (Stampin' Up)
Letter Brads (Provo Craft)
Letter Rub-ons (Making Memories)
Paper Clip (Karen Foster Designs)
Ribbon (Offray)
Tape (Therm-O-Web)
Zipper Pulls (Junkitz)

Page 43 Boots

Designer Polly McMillan

Cardstock
Label Maker (Dymo)
Letter Caps (Li'l Davis)
Patterned Papers (7gypsies, Karen Foster Designs)
Ribbon (Close to My Heart)
Safety Pins
Woven Labels (Me and My Big Ideas)

Patterned Papers (Chatterbox, DMD, KI Memories)
Round Corner Cutter
Square Punch (Marvy)
Stencil (Autumn Leaves)

Page 50 Puppy Wardrobe

Designer Stacey Panassidi

Fiber (FiberScraps)
Paper (Basic Grey)
Tags (Basic Grey)

Page 51 Puppy Dress Up

Designer Heather Preckel

Computer Font (Fancy Free from 2 Peas in a Bucket)
Label Maker (Dymo)
Letter Stickers (Kopp Design)
Patterned Papers (Kopp Design)
Ribbon (May Arts)
Tag (Kopp Design)

Page 52 Six Weeks

Designer Janine VanderHorst

Cardstock (Chatterbox)
Craft Paint (Making Memories)
Flower
Foam Stamps (Making Memories)
Letter Stickers (KI Memories)
Papers (Chatterbox)
Ribbon (Making Memories, May Arts)
Tacks (Chatterbox)

Page 52 Abbey's Dog

Designer Diana Furey

Brads (Boxer)
Computer Font (CK Journaling)
Flowers (Making Memories)
Frame (Making Memories)
Letter Charms (Making Memories)
Letters (Doodlebug)
Paper (Bo-Bunny, Chatterbox, Daisy D's)
Ribbon (Darice)
Rub-ons (SEI)

Page 54 Chewy

Designer Shannon Taylor

Charms (StampArts)
Cork Paper (Magic Scraps)
Decorative Chalks
Double-sided Tape (Therm-O-Web)
Jump Rings (Junkitz)
Patterned Papers (Paper Loft)
Ribbon (Li'l Davis)
Stamps (Fontwerks)
Transparency (Artistic Impressions)

Page 53 New Puppy

Designer Candace Leonard

Craft Paint (Making Memories)
Flower Brad (Making Memories)
Foam Stamps (Making Memories)
Ink (Ranger Inc.)
Papers (Making Memories)
Ribbon
Rub-ons (Li'l Davis, Making Memories)
Stamp (Postmodern Design)

Page 54 Meeting Wyatt

Designer Melanie Bauer

Cardstock (Bazzill)
Patterned Papers (K&Co.)
Pen (American Crafts)
Ribbon (Making Memories)
Rivets (Chatterbox)
Stickers (Sticko)

Page 54 Puppy Love

Designer Candace Leonard

Clip
Computer Font (Airplane from 2 Peas in a Bucket)
Craft Paint (Making Memories)
Negative (Creative Imaginations)
Papers (SEI)
Ribbon
Stamps (Making Memories)

Page 55 EveryBoy

Designer Candace Leonard

Computer Font (Evergreen from 2 Peas in a Bucket)
Craft Paint (Making Memories)
Frame (Making Memories)
Ink (Making Memories)

Papers (Basic Grey)
Ribbon
Stamps (Making Memories, Postmodern Design)

Page 56 Kyle & Cooper

Designer Sharon Geibig

Cardstock (Bazzill)
Computer Font (Monument from Chatterbox)
Date Stamp (Making Memories)
Foam Stamps (Making Memories)
Jewelry Tag
Paper (MAMBI)
Ribbon (Li'l Davis)
Twill Tape Ribbon
Wax Seal (Sonnets)

Page 57 Puppy Pick Up

Designer Candace Leonard

Cardstock
Computer Font (Tasklist from 2 Peas in a Bucket)
Craft Paint (Making Memories)
Epoxy Letters (Li'l Davis)
Foam Stamps (Making Memories)
Hole Renforcers
Ink (Ranger Inc.)
Letter Buttons (Junkitz)
Metal Frames (Li'l Davis)
Paper (KI Memories)
Photo Turns (7gypsies)
Ribbon
Rivets (Chatterbox)
Stamp (Postmodern Design)

Page 57 Woof

Designer Janine Vanderhorst

Cardstock (Bazzill, Chatterbox)
Craft Paint
Ink (Ranger Inc.)
Jump Rings (Junkitz)
Letter Stickers (Sonnets)
Machine Stitching
Metal Letter (Making Memories)
Moulding Strips (Chatterbox)
Paper (Chatterbox)
Ribbons (May Arts)
Silk Flower
Tag (Chatterbox)
Zipper Pulls (Junkitz)

Page 57 Love You

Designer Janine Vanderhorst

Blossom (Making Memories)
Button (Making Memories)
Canvas Tag (Art Warehouse)
Cardstock (Bazzill)
Hand-cut Stencil
Handmade Library Card
ID Plate (Art Warehouse)
Ink (Ranger Inc.)
Papers (Art Warehouse, KI Memories)
Ribbon (May Arts)
Rickrack (Wrights)
Safety Pin (Making Memories)
Machine Stitching
Transparency (Art Warehouse)
Zipper Pull (Junkitz)

Page 58 Slim Poses

Designer Erika Follansbee

Buttons (Making Memories)
Fonts (Mandingo, Arial)
Patterned Paper (KI Memories)

Page 59 Bath Time Kitty

Designer Melanie Baure

Bookplate (2 Peas in a Bucket)
Brads (Making Memories)
Cardstock (Bazzill)
Fiber
Ink (Ranger)
Patterned Paper (7gypsies, Chatterbox)
Stamps (Hero Arts)
Stickers (Creative Imaginations, Sticko,
    Stickopotomas)
Vellum (Chatterbox)

Page 60 You & Me

Designer Stacy Yoder

Cardstock (Bazzill)
Metal Letter (Making Memories)
Patterned Papers (7gypsies, Chatterbox,
    KI Memories)
Stencil Letters (Ma Vinci)

Page 61 Tiger

Designer Stacy Yoder

Craft Paint
Ink (Stampin' Up)
Letter Stamps (PSX)
Letter Stickers (Doodlebug,
    Sticker Studio)

Machine Stitching
Patterned Papers (Chatterbox,
    Kopp Designs)
Ribbon (Making Memories)
Stencil Number (Ma Vinci)
Word Plate (KI Memories)

Page 61 The Three Amigos

Designer Stacey Panassidi

Brads (Happy Hammer)
Cardstock (Bazzill)
Letters (Doodlebug)
Patterned Papers (Mustard Moon)
Stickers (EK Success)

Page 61 Chance

Designer Amy O'Neil

Brad
Cardstock (Bazzill)
Embossing Powder
Hinge
Patterned Papers (K&Co., Pebbles)
Ribbon (May Arts)
Rub-ons (Making Memories)
Tile (Junkitz)

Page 62 Sophie

Designer Heather Preckel

Cardstock
Computer Font (Unknown)
Letters (Doodlebug)
Patterned Papers (Daisy D's)
Ribbon (Li'l Davis)

Page 62 It's a Wrap

Designer Melanie Bauer

Cardstock (Bazzill)
Craft Paint (Making Memories)
Foam Stamps (Making Memories)
Ink (Clearsnap)
Patterned Papers (KI Memories,
    Scrapbook Wizard)
Pen (EK Success)
Photo Turns (Making Memories)
Ribbon (Making Memories)
Rub-ons (Making Memories)
Stamps (PSX)

Page 63 Gotcha

Designer Stacy Yoder

Brad
Buttons (Junkitz)
Cardstock (Bazzill)

Foam Stamps (Making Memories)
Ink (Stampin' Up)
Letter Stamps (PSX)
Patterned Papers (KI Memories)
Ribbon (Making Memories, May Arts)
Staples (Making Memories)

Page 63 Determination

Designer Stacy Yoder

Cardstock (Bazzill)
Craft Paint
Ink (Stampin' Up)
Number Stamps (PSX)
Patterned Papers (Chatterbox)
Ribbon (May Arts)
Stamps (Hot Potatoes)
Vellum Tags (Making Memories)
Washer Word (Making Memories)
Wire Flowers (Provo Craft)

Page 64 How Do I Love You?

Designer Angelia Wigginton

Buttons (Junkitz)
Cardstock
Computer Font (Hot Chocolate from
    2 Peas in a Bucket)
Heart Snaps (Making Memories)
Metal Bookplate (Making Memories)
Metal Letters (Making Memories)
Patterned Papers (Chatterbox)
Round Snaps (Making Memories)

Page 64 Lester

Designer Lee Anne Russell

Book Plates (Li'l Davis)
Brads
Buckle (Junkitz)
Cardstock
Computer Font (Tacoma)
Embroidery Floss (DMC)
Fabric Letters (Carolee's)
Ink (Stampin' Up)
Letter Buttons (Junkitz)
Patterned Papers (Chatterbox)
Ribbon

Page 65 Study Buddy

Designer Melanie Bauer

Cardstock (Bazzill)
Ink (Ranger Inc.)
Machine Stitching
Patterned Papers (Chatterbox)
Pen (EK Success)
Photo Corners (Making Memories)
Stamp (PSX)

Stickers (Creative Imaginations,
C-Thru Ruler, Mrs. Grossman's)
Tag (Making Memories)

Page 65 Jasper & Gracie

Designer Candace Leonard

Computer Font (High Tide
from 2 Peas in a Bucket)
Papers (Chatterbox, 7gypsies)
Twill (7gypsies)

Page 66 Location, Location, Location

Designer Melanie Bauer

Cardstock (Bazzill)
Paper Clip (Making Memories)
Patterned Papers (Chatterbox)
Pen (EK Success)
Ribbon (Offray)
Stickers (Sticko, Stickopotamus)

Page 66 Naming a Cat

Designer Melanie Bauer

Cardstock (Bazzill)
Computer Font (Another Typewriter)
Metal Frame (Making Memories)
Patterned Papers (KI Memories)
Stickers (Creative Imaginations)
Twine

Page 66 Magnetic

Designer Tonya Borrosch

Diecut Flower (Colorbok Photo
Graphics)
Label Maker (Dymo)
Patterned Papers (KI Memories)
Photo Corners (Making Memories)
Ribbon
Stencil (Autumn Leaves)
Sticker (American Crafts)

Page 67 See the Cat

Designer Elizabeth Ruuska

Cardstock (SEI)
Clipart (Dick and Jane)
Ink (Ranger, Inc.)
Jewelry Tags
Label Holder (Making Memories)
Letter Stamps (PSX)
Ribbon (Making Memories)
String

Page 68 Kitty Love

Designer Sharon Geibig

Cardstock (Bazzill)
Diecut Flowers (Colorbok)
Letter Stickers (Paperloft)
Paper Clip (7gypsies)
Papers (Chatterbox)
Ribbon (Making Memories)
Transparency (7gypsies)

Page 69 Thief of Hearts

Designer Erika Follansbee

Cardstock (Bazzill)
Computer Font (American Typewriter)
Flowers (KI Memories)
Letter Stickers (Creative Imagination)
Rub-ons (Making Memories)

Page 69 Caress the Tiger

Designer Melanie Bauer

Brads (Magic Scraps)
Buttons
Cardstock (Bazzill)
Ink (Ranger Inc.)
Stamps (Hero Arts, PSX)
Stickers (Creative Imaginations, Mrs.
Grossman's, Stickopotamus)
Tags (Avery)
Vellum (Chatterbox)
Yarn

Page 70 Fat Cat

Designer Lee Anne Russell

Embroidery Floss (DMC)
Fabric (Junkitz)
Jumping Rings (Junkitz)
Letter Buttons (Junkitz)
Machine Stitching
Patterned Papers (SEI)
Zipper (Junkitz)
Zipper Pull (Junkitz)

Page 70 Wise

Designer Melanie Bauer

Buttons (Junkitz)
Cat Button
Computer Font (American Typewriter)
Ink (Colorbok)
Patterned Papers (7gypsies, K&Co.,
Karen Foster Designs, Li'l Davis)
Screen

Page 72 Duchess

Designer Amy O'Neil

Cardboard Stencil Letter
Cardstock (Bazzil)
Computer Font (Georgia)
File Folder
Ink (Ranger Inc.)
Label Maker (Dymo)
Lace Trim
Letter Stamps (Rusty Pickle)
Micro Beads
Paper Doily
Patterned Papers (Anna Griffin,
Chatterbox, Mustard Moon)
Rhinestones

Page 72 Cats Are Like Potato Chips

Designer Shannon Taylor

Brads (Doodlebug Designs)
Chain Link (Magic Scraps)
Corrugated Cardboard
Fabric (Junkitz)
Gold Charm (Magic Scraps)
Hat Pin (Rusty Pickle)
Lace (Rusty Pickle)
Letter Rub-on (Making Memories)
Stamps (Hero Arts)
Tape (Therm-O-Web)
Textured Paper (Magic Scraps)
Transparency (Artistic Expressions)
Word Tag (Rusty Pickle)

Page 73 Cat or Gargoyle

Designer Sharon Geibig

Craft Paint (Making Memories)
Foam Stamps (Making Memories)
Letter Plate (K&Co.)
Letters (Foofala)
Metal Frame (K&Co.)
Papers (K&Co., Slab III)

Page 73 Funny Faces

Designer Melanie Bauer

Cardstock (Chatterbox)
Concho (Scrapworks)
Patterned Papers (Chatterbox, KI
Memories)
Pen (EK Success)
Stickers (Doodlebug)
Token (Doodlebug)

Papers (SEI)
Ribbon
Stamps (Ma Vinci)
Tag (Avery)
Vellum (SEI)

Page 84 Kiss & Hug

Designer Diana Furey

Brads (Bazzill)
Cardstock (Chatterbox)
Clay Tiles (Sweetwater)
Flowers (Making Memories)
Papers (Chatterbox, Sweetwater)
Ribbon (Darice)
Stamp
Wood Alphabet Letters (Li'l Davis)

Page 84 This Little Piggy

Designer Shannon Taylor

Bingo Letters (Li'l Davis)
Buttons (Junkitz)
Corrugated Paper
Craft Paint (Making Memories)
Decorative Chalk
Frame Nailheads (Scrapworks)
Letter Buttons (Junkitz)
Letter Run-ons (Making Memories)
Letter Stickers
Letter Template (EK Success)
Long Bars (7gypsies)
Metal Spiral
Patterned Paper (K&Co.)
Stamp (Paper Inspirations)
Stickers (Autumn Leaves,
    Mrs. Grossman's)
Tape (Therm-O-Web)

Page 85 Goat Barn

Designer Elizabeth Ruuska

Buckles (Junkitz)
Cardstock (Basic Gray, Close to My
    Heart, Club Scrap)
Clear Snap (Colorbok)
Ink (Colorbok, Ranger Inc.)
Letter Tool (QuicKutz)
Ribbon (Offray)
Stamps (A&P Numbers, Ma Vinci)

Page 86 See the Wonder

Designer Heather Prechel

Book Cloth (Chatterbox)
Computer Font (Wednesday from
    Chatterbox)
Molding Strip (Chatterbox)
Patterned Papers (Chatterbox)
Ribbon (Li'l Davis)
Rivets (Chatterbox)
Stitched Tag (Chatterbox)
Ticket Sticker (Li'l Davis)

Page 86 Ducks

Designer Heather Prechel

Cardstock (Bazzill)
Computer Font (Flower Pot from
    2 Peas in a Bucket)
Letter Buttons (Junkitz)
Ribbon (May Arts)

Page 87 Hi, Little Goat

Designer Amy O'Neil

Brads
Computer Fonts (Jesse James from
    Chatterbox, Man Print from
    Creating Keepsakes)
Ink (Ranger Inc.)
Large Slide Mount (Tempe Camera)
Pattern Papers (Daisy D's, Flair
    Designs)
Ribbon
Star Nailheads
Zipper Pull (Junkitz)

Page 87 Baby Calf

Designer Heather Prechel

Computer Font (Antique Type)
Patterned Papers (Chatterbox)
Ribbon (May Arts)
Stencil (Avery)

Page 88 Moo Cow

Designer Shannon Taylor

Adhesive
Brads (Creative Imaginations)

Ink (Stampin' Up)
Jump Rings (Junkitz)
Letters (Hoedown from
    ScrapVillage.com)
License Plate (Junkitz)
Ribbon (Offray)
Rubber Stamps (PSX)

Page 88 Dream Pony

Designer Diana Furey

Brads (Joanne's)
Cardstock (Bazzill)
Flowers (Li'l Davis, May Arts, Offray)
Hinges (Making Memories)
Letter Squares (Junkitz)
Machine Stitching
Ribbon (Li'l Davis, May Arts, Offray)
Tiles (Junkitz)
Transparency (Creative Imaginations)
Washer Words (Making Memories)

Page 88 Smile Goat

Designer Shannon Taylor

Buttons (Junkitz)
Chalks
Jute (Magic Scraps)
Label Maker (Dymo)
Letter Buttons (Junkitz)
Paper (Pebbles)
Patterned Transparency (Magic Scraps)
Stencil (Autumn Leaves)
Tape (Therm-O-Web)
Thick Embossing Enamel
    (Suze Weinberg)

Page 89 Barn Yard Miracle

Designer Annette Lauts

Buttons (Bazzill)
Cardstock (Bazzill)
Foam Stamps (Making Memories)
Machine Stitching
Number Stencil (Li'l Davis)
Patterned Papers (Chatterbox)
Ribbon
Rub-ons (Making Memories)
Stamps (Close to My Heart,
    Stampin' Up)
Zipper (Junkitz)
Zipper Pull (Junkitz)

Patterned Papers (KI Memories)
Ribbon (May Arts)
Stencil (Autumn Leaves)
Stickers (Sonnets, Nostalgiques)
Tags (KI Memories)

Page 98 Allergy Free Al

Designer Shannon Taylor

Brads (Doodlebug Designs)
Flat Embellishments (Scrappy Cat
    Creations)
Mesh
Patterned Papers (KI Memories)
Rub-ons (Creative Imaginations)
Tape (Therm-O-Web)

Page 98 Discover

Designer Heather Preckel

Cardstocks (Bazzill)
Label Maker (Dymo)
Ribbon (Li'l Davis, Offray)
Wood Flower (Li'l Davis)
Wood Frame (Li'l Davis)

Page 98 Molly & Kenny

Designer Renee Villalobos-Campa

Embroidery Floss (DMC)
Letter Buttons (Junkitz)
Letter Stickers (Artic Frog)
Machine Stitching
Patterned Papers (Artic Frog)

Page 99 Kissing Frogs

Designer Elizabeth Ruuska

Buttons (Junkitz)
Cardstock (KI Memories)
Corrugated Paper
Flower Button
Ink (Colorbok, Staz On)
Jewelry Pin
    (2 Peas in a Bucket)
Jumping Rings (Junkitz)
Labels (Junkitz)
License Plates (Junkitz)
Fabric Bows (Junkitz)
Patterned Papers (KI Memories)
Pens (American Crafts, Zig)
Safety Pin (Making Memories)
Snaps
Stamps (Antique Alphabet, PSX)
Tag (Junkitz)
Zipper (Junkitz)
Zipper Pull (Junkitz)

Page 100 Daisy

Designer Heather Preckel

Cardstock
Paper (KI Memories)
Ribbon (Offray)
Rub-ons (Making Memories)
Tag

Page 100 Macaw

Designer Amy O'Neil

Corrugated Cardboard
Craft Paint (Plaid)
Foam Letter Stamps (Making
    Memories, Walmart)
Ink (Ranger Ink)
Label Maker (Dymo)
Metal Letter Tag (Making Memories)
Patterned Paper (American Traditional,
    Flair Designs, K&Co.)
Ribbon
Safety Pins (Li'l Davis)
Twill
Zipper Pull (Junkitz)

Page 100 Franklin

Designer Heather Preckel

Cardstock
Computer Font (Wednesday
    from Chatterbox)
Label Maker (Dymo)
Diecut Letters (QuicKutz)
Paper (MAMBI)
Ribbon (Li'l Davis)
Staple
Tag (Avery)

Page 101 Turtle Crazy

Designer Angelia Wigginton

Bubble Letters (Li'l Davis)
Cardstock (Chatterbox)
Epoxy Letters (Creative Imaginations,
Making Memories)
Fabric Photo Corners (Canson, Making
    Memories)
Fiber (MAMBI)
Metal Frame (Li'l Davis)
Metal Letter (Making Memories)
Metal Stencil Letter
Patterned Paper (Chatterbox)
Ribbon (Making Memories)
Rub-ons (Creative Imaginations, Li'l
    Davis, Making Memories)
Silver Charm (Li'l Davis)
Snaps (Making Memories)
Tag (Making Memories)

Page 102 Found Turtle

Designer Shannon Taylor

Brads (Magic Scraps)
Computer Font
Diamond Glaze (Judikins)
Letter Stickers (American Traditional)
Metal Charms (Magic Scraps)
Patterned Paper (The Paper Loft)
Poem (2 Peas in a Bucket)
Ribbon (Me & My Big Ideas)
Tape (Therm-O-Web)
Textured Paper (Artistic Scrapper,
    Magic Scraps)

Page 102 Iggy

Designer Shannon Taylor

Bamboo Clips (Magic Scraps)
Cardstock
Craft Paint (Making Memories)
Lettering Template
Number Buttons (Junkitz)
Strings (Magic Scraps)
Sunshine Charm
Tape (Therm-O-Web)
Textured Papers

Page 103 Country Girl

Designer Annette Lauts

Cardstock (Bazzill)
Computer Font (CK Print)
Ink (Ranger Inc.)
Letters (QuicKutz)
Machine Stitching
Patterned Paper (Anna Griffin)
Photo Turns (7gypsies)
Wood Circle Letters (Li'l Davis
    Designs)

Page 103 Unexpected Beauty

Designer Debbie Hill

Note: Photos were altered in Photoshop to make the background black and white to bring out the colors of the snake.

Cardstock
Computer Fonts (Times New Roman)
Hinges (Making Memories)
Ink (Ink It)
Letters (QuicKutz)
Patterned Papers
Rub-ons (Making Memories)

Page104 Carter's Zoo

Designer Debbie Hill

Font (Squish from 2 Peas in a Bucket)
Patterned Paper (KI Memories)
Title Lettering (QuicKutz)

Page 105 Rhino or Dino

Designer Debbie Hill

Buckle (Junkitz)
Cardstock
Computer Font (Antique Type)
Metal Photo Corners (Making
    Memories)
Patterned Paper (Chatterbox)
Rub-ons (Autumn Leaves)

Page 106 My Dream Pet

Designer Shannon Taylor

Metal Ribbon Slides (Maya Road)
Patterned Paper (Rusty Pickle)
Ribbon (Making Memories)
Rub-ons (Creative Imaginations)
Stamps (PSX)
Tape (Therm-O-Web)

Page 106 Sea World

Designer Tony Barrosch

Cardstock (Bazzill)
Circle Cutter (Fiskars)
Fabric
Foam Stamps (Making Memories)
Ink (Ranger Inc.)
Letter Stamps (PSX)
Patterned Paper (Basic Grey)

Page 107   The Zoo

Designer Tonya Borrosch

Alphabet Stickers (Sticker Studio)
Cardstock (Bazzill)
Date Stamp
Label Maker (Dymo)
Mini Brads (Carolee)
Patterned Paper (Arctic Frog)
Pigment Ink (Color Box)
Ribbon (May Arts)
Tag

Page 107   2 Sleepy Pandas

Designer Amy O'Neil

Chipboard
Corner Foam Stamps (Making
    Memories)
Craft Paint (Plaid)
Embroidery Floss
Ephemera accent
Label Maker (Dymo)
Letter Buttons (Junkitz)
Letter Foam Stamps (Plaid)
Metal Number Two
Pattern Paper (NRN, Rusty Pickle)
Small Letter Stamps (EK Success)
Textured Cardstock (Bazzill)
Textured Strip (Magic Scraps)

Page 108 Elephants

Designer Amy O'Neil

Brad (Making Memories)
Cardboard Stencil
Cardstock (Bazzill)
Craft Paint (Plaid)
Ink (Ranger Inc.)
Letter Stamps (EK Success)
Pattern Paper (SEI)
Ribbon
Star Nail Heads

Page 108 Zoo Adventure

Designer Candace Leonard

Brad (Making Memories)
Cardstock
Envelopes (Chatterbox)
Foam Stamps (Making Memories)
Ink (Making Memories, Ranger Inc.)
Paint (Making Memories)
Papers (Chatterbox)
Ribbon (May Arts)
Rub-ons (Chatterbox)

Stamp (Postmodern Design, PSX,
    Stamp Studio)
Tags (Chatterbox)

Page 109 Brrr...

Designer Amy O'Neil

Cardstock (Bazzill)
Foam Letter Stamps (Making
    Memories)
Ink (Tsukineko)
Label Maker (Dymo)
Pattern Paper (Karen Foster Designs)
Ribbon (May Arts)
Round Zipper Pulls (Junkitz)
Snowflake Brads (Making Memories)

Page 110 Tiger Cubs

Designer Debbie Hill

Computer Fonts (Antique Type and
    Times New Roman)
Hand Cut Letters
Letters (QuicKutz)
Patterned Paper (Scrap Ease)

Page 111 Orangutan

Designer Tonya Borrosch

Brads
Computer Font (Verdana)
Letter Stickers (Artic Frog)
Letters (Foofala)
Map from Zoo
Number Stickers (Artic Frog)
Patterned Paper (Artic Frog)
Postage Stamps
Ribbon (May Arts)
Washer (Making Memories)

About the Author

As I write this "about the author" page, I think about how proud my mother is of me. She always told me that I wasn't using all of my natural talents. She was so right! Here is a bit of my story.

I spent most of my early adult years searching for myself. I worked in the garment industry from the time I was 20 years old. The job was in sales, as well as assisting the president of the company. My job satisfied me in many ways—I got to work with people, and I loved fashion. However it lacked in many other ways. There was no creative outlet for me. When I had my first child, my husband and I decided that I should stop working. We moved back to my home town to be close to my family, and I became a stay-at-home mom.

After having a career, I really missed working. I loved being home with my son, but I still longed to find myself! I was introduced to scrapbooking after the birth of my second son. A neighbor took me to a home scrapbooking party. I fell instantly in love! This was the hobby for me. It combined so many of the things I love—photography, color, design—plus I was preserving memories, which kept me connected to my family and my history.

I truly found myself immersed in this hobby. It fulfilled me in so many ways, except the business end. This is why I decided to start Junkitz. At the time, my husband was running a button business, and I felt that between the two of us we could start a business that was geared towards scrapbooking. I never in a million years would have thought that I would be able to get this business off the ground and made it the success that it has become. My husband has since closed his business and now works with me full time. We have our offices 5 minutes from our home, so my kids come to work often. I feel truly blessed that I have a job that I love. I have finally found myself in Junkitz, and you will find so much of me in our products. You will see my love for color, modern design, and my fashion influence in both our products and my scrapbooking style.

With that being said, I hope that you enjoy this book. It is a tribute to the other family members in our lives, our pets. I have two dogs, a black terrier mix named Snowball, and our new puppy, a Chihuahua named Scrappy. These animals give me comfort, relax me when I'm stressed, and provide endless playtime for my children. They too deserve to be included in our scrapbooks, for they are part of our history, and they make up our families. So, whether you have a dog, cat, pet pig, or simply many pictures from your local zoo or petting farm, you will find endless amounts of inspiration from the talented designers that contributed to this book.

–Stacey Panassidi

The End